STEVE BIDDULPH

MILLION COPY WORLDWIDE BESTSELLER

RAISING
BOYS

in the twenty-first century

NEW & UPDATED

How to help our boys
become open-hearted,
kind, strong men

Thorsons

Thorsons
An imprint of HarperCollins*Publishers*
1 London Bridge Street
London SE1 9GF

www.harpercollins.co.uk

First published in 1997 by Finch Publishing Pty Ltd, Australia
Revised and updated edition published in 2010 by HarperThorsons
This revised and updated edition 2018

5 7 9 10 8 6

Illustrations by Paul Stanish

Picture credits: p.3 © Anna Grigorjeva/Shutterstock.com; p.6 © Ulza/Shutterstock.com;
p.8 © Daisy Daisy/Shutterstock.com; p.10 © Keisuke N/Shutterstock.com (top),© Lopolo/
Shutterstock.com (bottom); p.11 © Monkey Business Images/Shutterstock.com; p.13 © The Light
Photography/Shutterstock.com; p.17 © Darren Baker/Shutterstock.com; p.24 © Dejan
Dundjerski/Shutterstock.com; p.26 © Dragon Images/Shutterstock.com; p.29 © Jack Frog/
Shutterstock.com; p.31 © Eakachai Leesin/Shutterstock.com; p.38 © Romrodphoto/Shutterstock.
com; p.44 © Fotokostic/Shutterstock.com; p.52 © Monkey Business Images/Shutterstock.com;
p.56 © Natalie Magic/Shutterstock.com; p.67 © Monkey Business Images/Shutterstock.com;
p.75 © Milicad/Shutterstock.com; p.88 © Treetree/Shutterstock.com; p.109 © Creatista/
Shutterstock.com; p.113 © I Am Nikom/Shutterstock.com; p.119 © Goodluz/Shutterstock.com;
p.125 © Oneinchpunch/Shutterstock.com; p.131 © Iakov Filimonov/Shutterstock.com;
p.146 © Monkey Business Images/Shutterstock.com; p.148 © KK Tan/Shutterstock.com;
p.155 © Brian A. Jackson/Shutterstock.com; p.158 © Monkey Business Images/
Shutterstock.com; p.172 © Twin Design/Shutterstock.com; p.175 © Rawpixel.com/
Shutterstock.com; p.179 © Lapina/Shutterstock.com; p.181 © Matimix/Shutterstock.com;
p.187 © Junpinzon/Shutterstock.com; p.189 © Rawpixel.com/Shutterstock.com

Permissions: The author gratefully acknowledges the permission of the following for the right
to reproduce copyright material in this publication: 'What Fathers Do' by Jack Kammer
(pp.80–83), is reprinted from *Full-Time Dads*, May/June 1995 Issue, with the permission of
the author; six myths of porn (p.136) is reprinted from Elizabeth Clark, *Love, Sex and
No Regrets for Today's Teens* (Finch, Sydney, 2017).

A catalogue record of this book is
available from the British Library

ISBN 978-0-00-828367-4

Printed and bound in Great Britain by
CPI Group (UK) Ltd, Croydon CR0 4YY

MIX
Paper from
responsible sources
FSC® C007454

Contents

Boyhood Has Changed 1

1 What Is It with Boys? 5

2 The Three Stages of Boyhood 9

3 Testosterone 39

4 Making a New Kind of Man 59

5 What Dads Can Do 71

6 Mothers and Sons 97

7 Developing a Healthy Sexuality 121

8 Out into the Big World 143

9 Boys and Sport 177

10 A Community Challenge 189

Notes 203

Appendix: Do Gender Differences Exist, and Do They Matter? 211

Boyhood Has Changed

Boyhood is transforming; that's it in a nutshell. If you've been in any school gate or online conversations in the past twenty years, you'll know that things are on the move. We're learning how to make boyhood a happier place, and that knowledge is saving lives.

The book you hold in your hand had a very interesting effect that echoed around the world – it was as if a million mothers and fathers all at once gave an enormous sigh of relief. (Our boy is normal!) For one thing, the book cut through the endless argument between nature and nurture by saying, 'It's both.' But nurture is the one we can do something about, so let's get started.

In a world where so many boys struggled, there was a desperate need for a new approach. *Raising Boys* provided that. It said that if we want boys to grow into truly good men with warm hearts and strong backbones, then we have to understand their specific needs. Just as with girls, specific risk factors go with being an average boy. These range from the everyday to the truly terrible – from not liking school at four, to having three times the risk of dying in their teens (mostly from car accidents, suicide or violence) and nine times the chance of going to jail.[1] These are not small things. But if we understand what makes our boys unique, we can love them better and make sure they turn out well.

Today we understand that gender is on a continuum. Knowing a child is a boy or a girl doesn't tell you anything, necessarily, about what they will be like. But although gender is a line, there are big bumps on that line, and so we can say 'most' boys and 'most' girls without meaning it has to apply to all. Most boys are slower at learning to talk, and being ready to read or write, than most girls. Most start puberty a year or two later than girls. (Girls' puberty is over by fourteen, and they have shot up to their full height. Boys' puberty doesn't end until they are about seventeen, and their brains don't fully mature until their twenties.) These things matter if you have a boy to raise, and keep alive.

The differences are not just on the outside. The evidence grows and grows that boys' chemistry is very different from early in the womb, predisposing most of them to greater muscle mass, more need for movement and activity, an excitement about competition, and a love of concrete ways of learning. Though there are definitely some girls who are like this, and boys who are not. Keep remembering that mantra – *most, not all.*

Boys' brains develop more slowly, and their nervous system wires up in a different sequence, and that is a massive thing because it means that in the UK and Australia, they start school far too young, and often hate it because it's too formal, too much based on sitting still. Good schools for boys are the ones that give them room to move and time to grow.

There are other great changes afoot. Understanding that some boys are gay or transgender and that's normal and OK has helped millions of parents to be more relaxed and accepting of their own unique boy. In fact, it's made every boy and girl a lot freer to be themselves. Less homophobia means that all boys can have warm friendships, cry when they are sad, be affectionate, and have much better mental health as a result.

Knowing about the autism spectrum has also brought great relief to millions of parents and kids. We can all relax about being a little bit – or very – different. We are valuing and accepting kids who don't quite fit the mould.

Of course, there is so much more in this book. The three stages of boyhood. How to keep boys safe. Boys and housework! And the powerful message that men have an equal part to play in raising children. Kids need to know men of every kind – creative, practical, brave, shy, funny, of every different race, sexuality and type. Then boys can base their own masculinity on a broad choice of role models. And girls can see every possible kind of man.

Right now, the world badly needs good men. There are some awful ones needing to be put in their place. Your boy can be one of those who grow up so much better, and help to heal this sad and scary world. Thank you for joining the boy revolution. As the twenty-first century rolls on, it's badly needed.

Enjoy your boy, love him well, and watch him fly in his own special way.

Steve Biddulph

AN IMPORTANT NOTE

The aim of this book is to help you think – and feel – deeply about your job of being a parent. Treat it as a springboard. But don't treat it as a prescription. Nobody can tell you how to raise your child, and if you ever see the words 'parenting expert' you should run a mile. I am not one of those, and I simply offer these thoughts to help you figure out your own.

Parenthood is hard. We shouldn't have to feel alone. We should support each other at every opportunity. I hope this book really helps.

Steve B.

Chapter 1

What Is It with Boys?

Last night I drove into town for a meeting, or at least tried to, and the situation with young men was once again thrust into my face. Three cars ahead of me, the Pacific Highway was blocked. A car driven by a teenage boy, with four friends on board, had attempted to pull out into the traffic, but miscalculated. A truck coming up behind had hit the car and carried it 50 metres along the road, badly crushing it in the impact. Soon the emergency vehicles arrived: fire, police, ambulance. People worked in teams, calmly but rapidly dealing with the situation.

The young driver was gradually cut out of the wreck unconscious. His four male passengers had varying injuries, some serious. An older woman, perhaps the mother of one of the boys, came running from a nearby farm. A policeman gently comforted her. Maleness was everywhere – inexperience and risk on the one side; compe-tence, caring and steadiness on the other.

It kind of summed up for me the male situation. Men, when they turn out well, are wonderful – selfless, heroic, hardworking. But being young and male is so vulnerable, so prone to disaster. When we see a boy born these days, we can't help wondering – how will he turn out? Back in the twentieth century boys started out OK – little boys were full of life and love, trusting and close to their mums and dads, laughing and free. But on starting school they often became tense and unhappy. Soon they were roaming the playground in gangs, harassing girls and bullying smaller boys. By their teens they were shut down, gruff and grunting, unpleasant to be around. And often they turned into dull and difficult men, sexually incompetent wage slaves with no real friendships, no sense of joy, blotting it all out with beer and sport. Masculinity a generation back was a pretty sad place. Now that is changing.

Where are you up to with your boy or boys? Perhaps you are reading this with a little baby boy newly arrived in your life. Perhaps you have a noisy toddler, thankfully now asleep in his room, looking all innocent in his sleep! Or a boy at school, a mixture of brave and vulnerable as he faces the world on his own terms, but still races back to you for comfort and guidance.

Please – take it from me – the years will rush by, and one day you will be watching your son as a man, and feeling incredibly proud that he is caring, safe, making a contribution, and hopefully going far beyond you in the scope of his life.

This will be the generation when we create a new kind of man in such numbers that the world is turned around. That's been the purpose of my life, and I hope it will be yours too.

The Good Stuff to Come

In this book we will look at many breakthrough areas of understanding boys. In the next chapter we'll start by explaining their three distinct stages of development:

- zero to six – the learning to love years
- six to fourteen – the time when fathers count most, and
- fourteen to adult – when boys need mentors and adults who care, in addition to their parents.

By knowing these stages, you will be prepared and more relaxed about what is coming next and how to deal with it.

In the third chapter, we'll examine the effects of hormones on boys' behaviour, and how to help boys ride these powerful waves of development. Everyone knows about hormones, but when do they actually come into action, and what do they do? Why are thirteen-year-olds often dopey and fourteen-year-olds so argumentative? And how do you handle this with understanding and maintain your sense of humour?

In Chapter 4 we'll show how a new kind of boy is emerging in the twenty-first century who can show his emotions, cry without being ashamed and communicate clearly and well. A boy with backbone and heart, able to step away from the old toxic and unhappy forms of masculinity and be loving and close.

Next comes the vital place of fathers, and how to get it right even if your own father wasn't all that great. Most men, it seems, want to improve on the way their fathers were, but don't always know how. The fatherhood revolution is one of the most positive developments of the past thirty years. If you are a single mum reading this, we will also tell you what you can do to ensure your son has good men in his life.

Then come some stories and clues about mothers and sons. Mothers need to be confident and proactive with their boys, helping them to feel OK around the opposite sex. A mum is a 'practice girl-friend', and she teaches a boy how to get along happily with women.

Whether she knows it or not, she is setting the pattern for all his future relationships.

Next we'll talk about boys and sex, since this is a vital area that can make their lives happy or miserable, depending on how it's handled.

Then – since school is where boys spend half their childhoods, there's a chapter on how schools can be dramatically improved. We will also help you decide which teachers and which school will best help your boy.

To round things off, we'll tackle sport, which can be hazardous to boys' bodies and souls – though when it's done right it can be so good for them. Boys need sport, so we need sport to get its act together.

And lastly, we'll discuss the ways in which the whole community can support boys turning into men – because parents can't do this without help. Parents need to be making choices even when their boys are still little babies, to ensure other adults are there for the boys as they navigate their teens. You need a circle of friends and an extended family to help a boy make it to adulthood unharmed. Interested? Mystified? Then it's time to begin.

Boys can be just great. We can make them so. Understanding is the key.

Chapter 2

The Three Stages of Boyhood

Have you ever browsed through a family photo collection and seen photos of a boy growing up, from babyhood right through to manhood? If you have, you'll know that boys don't grow up in a smooth way. They go in surges – looking the same for a while, then suddenly appearing to change overnight. And that's only on the outside. On the inside, great changes are happening, too. But developing maturity and character aren't as automatic as physical development; a boy can get stuck. Everyone knows at least one man who is large in body but small in mind or soul, who hasn't developed as a mature person. Such men are everywhere – they might be a prime minister, a president or a tycoon, but you look at them and think, *Yep, still a boy. And not a very nice one …*

Boys don't grow up well if you don't help them. You can't just shovel in cereal, provide clean T-shirts, and have them one day wake up as a man! A certain programme has to be followed. The trick is to understand what is needed – and when.

Luckily, boys have been around for a very long time. Every society in the world has encountered the challenge of raising boys, and has come up with solutions. The three stages of boyhood are timeless and universal. Native Americans, Kalahari bushmen and Inuit hunters all knew about these stages. When I talk about them to parents they say, 'That's right!' because the stages match their experience.

The Three Stages at a Glance

1. The first stage of boyhood is from *birth to six*, the span of time when – in most families – the boy primarily belongs to his mother. He is 'her' boy, even though his father may play a very big role, too. The aim at this age is to give strong love and security and to 'switch a boy on' to life as a warm and welcoming experience.

2. The second stage includes the years from *six to fourteen* – when the boy, out of his own internal drives, starts wanting to learn to be a man and looks more and more to his father for interest and activity (although his mother remains very involved, and the wider world is beckoning, too). The purpose of this stage is to build competence and skill while also developing kindness and playfulness – you help him to

become a balanced person. This is the age when a boy becomes happy and secure about being male.

3. Finally, the years from *fourteen to adult* – when the boy needs input from male mentors if he is to complete the journey to being fully grown-up. Mum and Dad step back a little, but they must organise some good mentors in their son's life; if not, he will have to rely on an ill-equipped peer group for his sense of self. The aim is for your son to learn skills, responsibility and self-respect by joining more and more with the adult community.

These stages do not indicate a sudden or sharp shift from one parent to another. It's not like the mum stage, the dad stage and the mentor stage. For instance, an involved dad can do a huge amount from birth onwards, or even take the role a mother usually has if need be. And a mother doesn't quit when a boy reaches six – quite the opposite. The stages indicate a shift in emphasis: the father 'comes to the fore' more from six to thirteen, and the importance of mentors increases from fourteen onwards. In a sense, it's about adding new ingredients at each stage.

The three stages help us know what to do. For example, we know that fathers of boys from six to fourteen must not be just busy work-aholics, or absent themselves emotionally or physically from the family. If they do, this will certainly damage their sons. (Yet most fathers of the twentieth century did just that – as many of us can remember from our own childhood.)

The stages tell us that we must look for extra help from the community when our sons are in their mid-teens – the role that used to be taken by extended family members (uncles and grandfathers) or by the tradesman–apprentice relationship. Too often, teenagers move outwards into the big world but no one is there to catch them, and they spend their teens and early adulthood in a dangerous half-way stage, with only peers to depend on.

It's a fair bet that many problems with boys' behaviour – poor school motivation, depression, young men getting into trouble with the law (drink-driving, fights, crime, etc.) – have escalated because we haven't known about these stages and provided the right human ingredients at the right times.

The stages are so important that we must look at each of them in more detail and decide how to respond. That's what we'll do now.

From Birth to Six: The Gentle Years

Babies are babies. Whether they are a boy or girl is not a concern to them, and needn't be to us, either. Babies love to be cuddled, to play, to be tickled and to giggle; to explore and to be swooshed around. Their personalities vary a lot. Some are easy to handle, quiet and relaxed, and sleep long hours. Others are noisy and wakeful, always wanting some action. Some are anxious and fretful, needing lots of reassurance that we are there and that we love them.

What all babies and toddlers need most is to form a special bond with at least one person. Usually this person is their mother. Partly because she is the one who is most willing and motivated, partly because she provides the milk, and partly because she tends to be cuddly, restful and soothing in her approach, a mother is usually the best equipped to provide what a baby needs. Her own hormones (especially prolactin, which is released into her bloodstream as she breastfeeds) prime her to want to be with her child and to give it her full attention.[1]

Except for breastfeeding, dads can provide all a baby needs. But dads tend to do it differently: studies show them to be more vigorous

in their playing[2] – they like to stir children up, while mothers like to calm them down (although if fathers get as deprived of sleep as mothers sometimes do, they too will want to calm baby down!).

Learning to Love

If a mother is the main caregiver, a boy will see her as his first model for intimacy and love. If she builds this close bond, then from toddlerhood on – if she sets limits with her son firmly but without hitting or shaming him – he will take this in his stride. He will want to please her, and will be easier to manage because the attachment is so strong. He knows he has a special place in her heart. Being made to wait or to change his behaviour might baffle him, but he will get over it. He knows he's loved, and he will not want to displease the person at the centre of his existence.

Mum's interest and fun in teaching and talking to him helps his brain to develop more verbal skills and makes him more sociable. Boys need more help than girls to catch on to social skills (more on this later).

If a mother is terribly depressed, and therefore unresponsive in the first year or two of her son's life, his brain may undergo physical changes and become a 'sad brain'.[3] If she is constantly angry, hitting or hurting him, he will be confused over whether she loves him. (Please note, this is constant anger we are talking about, not occasional rattiness that all parents feel and show. We aren't supposed to be angels as parents – if we are, how would our children learn about the real world?)

Those of us who are around young mothers have to be careful to support and help them, to ensure they are not left isolated or overwhelmed with physical tasks. A mother needs others to augment her life so she can relax and do this important work. If we care for young mothers, they can care for their babies. Husbands and partners are the first rank of help, but family and neighbours are also needed.

What Goes On Between Mother and Baby Boy?

Science has trouble measuring something like love, but it's getting better. Scientists studying mothers and babies have observed what they call 'joint attention sequences'. This is love in action, love you can see. You will have certainly experienced this with your own child. The baby seeks out your attention with a gurgle or cry. You look towards him and see that he is looking at you. He is thrilled to make eye contact, and wiggles with delight. You talk back to him. Or maybe you are holding him or changing him, and you feel that closeness as you sing to or tickle him. He impacts on you, and you on him. The exchange goes on, a 'pre-words' conversation – it's delightful and warm. Researchers filmed mothers and babies going about their day, and discovered that joint attention sequences happen between 50 and 100 times a day.[4] This is where the ability to relate to others skilfully and sensitively is first learnt.

Another kind of joint attention sequence is when a child is distressed and you croon, stroke or hold him gently, and distract him – you care for him based on your growing experience of what works to help him calm down. Or you engage with him just to enjoy seeing him become happy or excited. Soon your 'joint attention' might be directed at a toy, a flower, an animal or a noise-making object that you enthuse about together. You are teaching him to be interested in his world.

This is one of the most significant things a parent ever does for their baby. Inside baby's little head, his brain is sprouting like broccoli in the springtime. When a baby is happy, growth hormone flows through his body and right into his brain, and development blossoms. When he is stressed, the stress hormone – cortisol – slows down growth, especially brain growth. So interaction, laughter and love are like food for a baby's brain. All this interaction is being remembered in these new brain areas: the baby is learning how to read faces and moods, be sensitive, and learn calmness, fun, stern admonition or warm love. Soon he will be adding language, music, movement, rhythm and, above all, the capacity for feeling good and being empathic with other people. Boy babies are just a little slower, a little less wired for sociability than girls, and so they especially need this help. And they need it from someone who knows them very well, who has the time and who is themselves reasonably happy and content.

The process keeps going right into little-boyhood. A mother shows delight when her child makes mud pies, and admires his achievements. His father tickles him and play-wrestles with him, and is also gentle and nurturing, reading stories and comforting him when he is sick. The little boy learns that men are kind as well as exciting, that dads read books and are capable in the home; and that mothers are kind but also practical, and part of the bigger world.

In Short

To sum up, the first lessons boys need to learn are in closeness – shown through trust, warmth, fun and kindness. Under six years of age, gender isn't a big deal, and it shouldn't be made so. Mothers are usually the primary parent, but a father can also take this place. What matters is that one or two key people love the child and make him central for these few years. That way, he develops inner security for life, and his brain acquires the skills of intimate communication and a love of life and the world. These years are soon over. Enjoy your little boy while you can!

From Six to Fourteen: Learning to Be Male

At around six years of age, a big change takes place in boys. There seems to be a 'switching on' of boys' masculinity at this age. Even boys who have not watched any television suddenly want to play with swords, wear Superman capes, fight and wrestle and make lots of noise.[5] Something else happens that is really important: it's been observed in all societies around the world. At around six years of age, little boys seem to 'lock on' to their dad, or stepdad, or whichever male is around, and want to be with him, learn from him and copy him. They want to study how to be male.

If a dad ignores his son at this time, the boy will often launch an all-out campaign to get his attention. Once I consulted in the case of a little boy who repeatedly became seriously ill for no apparent reason. He was placed in intensive care. His father, a leading medical specialist, flew back from a conference overseas to be with him, and the boy got better. The father went away to another conference, and the illness came back. That's when they called in the psychologists. We asked the father to reconfigure his lifestyle, which involved being on the road for eight months a year. He did this, and the boy has not been ill since.

YA HOLD YA ARMS LIKE THIS !

Boys may steal, break things, act aggressively at school and develop any number of problem behaviours just to get Dad to take an interest. But if Dad is already in there on a daily basis playing, teaching and caring for his son, then this stage will go smoothly.

Mums Still Matter Just as Much

This sudden shift of interest to the father does not mean that Mum leaves the picture. In the past, in North America and the UK especially, mothers would often distance themselves from their boys at this age, to 'toughen them up'. (This was also the age that the British upper classes sent their boys to boarding school.) But as Olga Silverstein has argued in her book, *The Courage to Raise Good Men*,[6] this often backfired. If, in the early years, a mother suddenly withdraws her presence or her warmth and affection, then a terrible thing happens: the boy, to control his grief and pain, shuts down the part of him that connects with her – his tender and loving part. He finds it just too painful to feel loving feelings if they are no longer reciprocated by his mother. If a boy shuts down this part of him, he will have trouble as an adult expressing warmth or tenderness to his own partner or children, and will be a rather tense and brittle man.[7] We all know men like this (bosses, fathers, even husbands) who are emotionally restricted and awkward with people. We can make sure our sons are not like this by hugging them, talking to them, listening to their feelings, whether they are five, ten or fifteen.

Mothers have to stay constant, while being willing to let Dad also play his part. Boys need to know they can count on Mum, in order to keep their tender feelings alive. Things work best if they can stay close to Mum, but add Dad, too. If a dad feels a child is too taken up with his mother's world (which can happen), he should increase his own involvement – not criticise the mother! Sometimes a dad is too critical or expects too much, and the boy is afraid of him. A father might have to learn to be more thoughtful, gentler, or just more fun, if his son is to successfully cross the bridge into manhood with him.

The six- to fourteen-year-old boy still adores his mother, and has plenty to learn from her. But his interests are changing – he is becoming more focused on what men have to offer. A boy knows that he is turning into a man. He has to 'download the software' from an available male to complete his development.

The mother's job is to relax about this, and stay warm and supportive. The father's job is to progressively step up his involvement. If there is no father around, then the child depends more on finding other men – at school, for instance.

PRACTICAL HELP

WHAT TO DO IF YOU'RE A SINGLE MOTHER

For thousands of years, single mothers have needed to raise boys without a man in the house. And more often than not, these boys have turned out just great. Please take this on board right away – mums on their own can raise fine men.

Over the years I have interviewed mothers who did this, to find out their secret. Successful single mothers of sons always give the same advice. Firstly, they found good male role models, calling in help from uncles, good friends, schoolteachers, sports coaches, youth leaders and so on (choosing with care to guard against the risk of sexual abuse). A boy needs to know what a good man looks like. If caring men are involved enough, and over a sufficiently long period of time, this provides that one missing thing a mother can't give – a male example to copy. If there are one or two good men who know and care about your son, it makes a huge difference. (It's the same if you are in a two-mother family, raising a boy. There will be men in your social circle who are the kind of man you would want your son to emulate. Ask them to get involved.)

Single mums can also comfort themselves that, after all, many boys with dads only see them for basically a few minutes a day. Whatever you do, don't marry some deadbeat just so your son can have a man in the house!

Part of the survival kit of single mothers is the network(s) of good men in their community. If you are a dad, your son will certainly have friends who don't have a dad present or whose dad is not very involved. Think about inviting that boy when you plan a trip to a concert, the beach, a sports game or a weekend away with your own son. His mum will be so appreciative, though she would never have asked for this, not wanting to impose. (She may be a little cautious, so perhaps don't start with a nine-day wilderness trek.)

Single parents need to be networked. Being involved in a community group, church, sporting or hobby group, extended family, or just a neighbourhood where kids are loved and valued is a natural way to provide other good adult role models and people to bounce off, especially in adolescence.

There's one more thing. All the successful single parents I've known also recognised they needed to be kind to themselves, and not become long-suffering martyrs. (Martyrdom is like yoghurt: it has a shelf life of maybe two weeks, then it tends to go kind of sour!) Single parents who did well planned into their lives a massage, a game of racquetball, a yoga class, or just time vegging out watching television when the children were asleep – and they kept this commitment to their own wellbeing. (For more help on single parenting, see also page 109.)

FIVE FATHERING ESSENTIALS

All fathers have one thing in common: they would like to be good dads. The problem is, if we weren't given great fathering ourselves, and many of us weren't, how do you turn good intentions into action? What if you just never got the 'software'? The best way is to hang around other men and learn from what they do, see what you would copy and what you would never repeat! From talking to hundreds of men, here are five basic clues.

1. *Start early.* Be involved in the pregnancy – talk with your partner about your hopes for the child and your plans and dreams for how you want your family to be. Plan to be at the birth – and stick to the plan! Go to some birth classes, especially those just for fathers, which are being offered more and more. Once your baby is born, get involved in baby care right from the start. Have a speciality. Bathing is good: they are slippery little suckers, but it's a fun time and a big help. This is the key time for relationship-building. Caring for a baby 'primes' you hormonally and alters your life priorities. So beware! Fathers who care for babies physically start to get fascinated and very in tune with them – it's called 'engrossment'. Men can become the expert at getting babies back to sleep in the middle of the night – walking them, bouncing, singing gently, or whatever works for you! Don't settle for being useless around babies – keep at it, get support and advice from the baby's mother and other experienced friends. And take pride in your ability. If you have a demanding career, use your weekends or holidays to get immersed in your child. From when your child is two, encourage your partner to go away for the weekend with her girlfriends and leave you and your toddler alone, so that both you and she know you are capable and can 'do it all'. Try to clean up before she gets home – this really impresses spouses.

2. *Make time.* This is the bottom line, so listen closely. For fathers, this may be the most important sentence in this whole book: *if you routinely work a fifty-five- or sixty-hour week, including commute times, you just won't cut it as a dad.* Your sons will have problems in life, your daughters will have self-esteem issues, and it will be down to you. Fathers need to get home in time to play, laugh, teach and tickle their children. Corporate life, and also small business, can be enemies of the family. Often fathers find the answer is to accept a lower income and be around their family more. Next time you're offered a promotion involving longer hours and more nights away from home, seriously consider telling your boss, 'Sorry, my kids come first.'

3. *Show your love.* Hugging, holding and playing tickling and wrestling games can take place right through to adulthood! Do gentler things, too – kids respond to quiet storytelling, sitting together, singing or playing music. Tell your kids how great, beautiful, creative and intelligent they are (often, and with feeling). If your parents were not demonstrative, you will just have to learn. Some dads fear that cuddling their son will turn him into a 'sissy'. In fact, the reverse is probably true. Sons whose dads are affectionate and playful with them will be closer to their fathers, want to emulate them more, and be comfortable in the company of men. For both sons and daughters, a dad's affection is vital. A child can't understand that you work long hours, worry over tax forms or scrimp and save for his future, because that's not something he can see or touch. Kids know they are loved through touch and eye contact and laughter and fun. Affection is reassuring – it conveys love in a way that words cannot. Children who are hugged and kissed feel safer in the world, and when Dad does it too, they are doubly secure.

4. *Lighten up.* Enjoy your kids. Being with them out of guilt or obligation is second-rate – they sense you are not really there in spirit. Experiment to find those activities that you both enjoy. Take the pressure to achieve off your kids: when you play a sport or game, don't get into too much heavy coaching or competition.

Remember to laugh and muck about. Only enrol them in one, or at most two organised sports or activities, so they have time to just 'be'. Reduce racing-around time, and devote it instead to walks, games and conversations. Avoid over-competitiveness in any activity beyond what is good fun. Teach your kids, continuously, everything you know.[8]

5. *Heavy down.* Some fathers today are lightweight 'good-time' dads who leave all the hard stuff to their partners. After a while of this, these partners start to say, 'I have three kids, and one of them is my husband.' There is an unmistakable indicator for this – when your sex life declines badly!

Get involved in the decisions and discussions in the kitchen, help to supervise homework and housework. Develop ways of discipline that are calm but definite. Don't hit – although with young children you may have to gently hold and restrain them from time to time. Don't shout if you can help it. Aim to be the person who stays calm, keeps things on track, and pushes the discussion on about how to solve behaviour problems. You are your children's guide. through your clarity, focus and experience, not through being bigger and meaner. Do listen to your kids, and take their feelings into account.

Talk with your partner about the big picture: 'How are we doing overall? What changes are needed?' Parenting as a team can add a new bond between you and your partner. Check with your partner if you are stuck or don't know how to react. You don't have to have all the answers – no one does. Parenthood is about making mistakes, fixing them, and moving right along.

In Short

All through the primary school years and into mid-high school, boys should spend a lot of time with their fathers and mothers, gaining their help, learning how to do things, and enjoying their company. From an emotional viewpoint, the father is now more significant. The boy is ready to learn from his dad, and listens to what he has to say. Often he will take more notice of his father. It's enough to drive a mother wild!

This window of time – from about age six to the fourteenth birthday – is the major opportunity for a father to have an influence on (and build the foundations of masculinity in) his son. Now is the time to 'make time'. Little things count: playing in the backyard on summer evenings; going for walks and talking about life and telling him about your own childhood; working on hobbies or sports together, just for the enjoyment of doing it. This is when good memories are laid down, which will nourish your son, and you, for decades to come.

Don't be deterred if your son acts 'cool', as he has learnt to do this from his schoolmates. Persist and you will find a laughing, playful boy just under the surface. Enjoy this time when he really is wanting to be with you. By mid-adolescence his interests will pull him more and more into the wider world beyond. All I can do here is plead with you – don't leave it too late!

Fourteen and Onwards: Becoming a Man

At around fourteen years of age a new stage begins. Usually by now a boy is growing fast, and a remarkable thing is happening on the inside – his testosterone levels have increased by almost 800 per cent over his pre-puberty amount![9]

Although every boy is different, it's common for boys at this age to get a little argumentative, restless and moody. It's not that they are turning bad – it's just that they are being born into a new self, and any type of birth always involves some struggle. They are needing to find answers to big questions, to begin new adventures and challenges, and to learn competencies for living – and their body clock is urging them on.

I believe this is the age when we fail kids the most. In our society, all we offer the mid-teens is 'more of the same': more school, more of the routines of home. But the adolescent is hungry for something else, something new. He is hormonally and physically ready to break out into an adult role, but we want him to wait another four or five years! It's little wonder that problems arise.

What's needed is something that will engage the spirit of a boy – that will pull him headlong into some creative effort or passion that gives his life wings. All the things that parents have nightmares about (adolescent risk-taking, alcohol, drugs, unsafe sex and criminal activity) happen because we do not find channels for young men's desire for glory and heroic roles. Boys look at the larger society and see little to believe in or join in with. Even their rebellion is

packaged up and sold back to
them by advertisers and the
music industry. They want to
jump somewhere better and
higher, but that place is nowhere
in sight.

SON, I'VE FIXED
THE TRAIN SET !

What Old Societies Did

In every society before ours –
from the tropics to the poles
– in every time and place that
has been studied by anthropol-
ogists, mid-teen boys received
a burst of intensive care and
attention from the whole
community. This was a universal human activity, so it must have
been important. These cultures knew something we are still learning – that parents cannot raise teenage boys without getting the
help of other adults.

One reason for this is that fourteen-year-old sons and their
fathers drive each other crazy. Often it's all a father can manage
to love his son. Trying to do this and teach him can be just impossible. (Remember your dad teaching you to drive?) Somehow the
two males just get their horns tangled and make each other worse.
Fathers get too intense: they feel they are running out of time as a
dad, and they see their own mistakes being repeated.

Once, when I was an inexperienced family therapist, we saw a
family whose fourteen-year-old teenage son had run away and lived
in the railway yards for several days. He was found, but it scared
everyone, and the family felt they needed to get help. Talking to
them, we discovered a remarkable thing. Sean was their youngest
son, but he wasn't the first to do this running away thing! Each of
their three sons had 'done a runner' around this age. My boss, a
wise and scarily intuitive man, looked the father straight in the eye.
'Where did you go when you were fourteen?' The father pretended
not to understand but, with his entire family looking accusingly

on at him, grinned foolishly and spilled the beans. He had been a teenage runaway at fourteen after huge fights with his dad. He'd never told his wife about this, let alone his kids. Without knowing it, though, he had become increasingly impossible, uptight and picky as his own sons reached that age. Effectively, unconsciously, he drove them to run away. Luckily, the family tradition called for coming home again, safe and sound.

So fathers and fourteen-year-old sons can get a bit tense with each other. If someone else can assist with the male role at this age, then dads and sons can relax a little. (Some wonderful movies have been based on this – look out for *Searching for Bobby Fisher*, *Finding Forrester* and *The Run of the Country*, or all three seasons of the TV series *Newsroom*.)

Traditionally, two things were done to help young men into adulthood. First, they were 'taken on' and mentored into adulthood by one or more men who cared about them and taught them important skills for living. And second, at certain stages of this mentoring process, the young men were taken away by the community of older men and initiated. This meant being put through some serious growing-up processes, including testing, sacred teaching and new responsibilities. We'll come back to this in the final chapter, on community.

We can contrast initiations such as the Lakota experience (see page 32) with many modern-day sons and their mothers, who (according to writers like Babette Smith in *Mothers and Sons*[10]) often remain in an awkward, distant or rather infantile relationship for life. These sons fear getting too close, and yet, being uninitiated as men, they never really escape. Instead, they relate to all women in a dependent and immature way. Not having entered the community of men, they are distrustful of other men and have few real friends. They are afraid of commitment to women because for them it means being mothered, and that means being controlled. They are real 'nowhere men'.

It's only by leaving the world of women that young men can break the mother-mould and relate to women as fellow adults. Domestic violence, unfaithfulness and the inability to make a marriage work may result not from any problem with women but from men's failure to take boys on this transforming journey.

You might think that (in the old societies) the boys' mothers, and perhaps the fathers too, would resent or fear their son being 'taken over' by others. But this was not the case. The initiators were men they had known and trusted all their lives. The women understood and welcomed this help, because they sensed the need for it. They were giving up a rather troublesome boy and getting back a more mature and integrated young man. And they were probably very proud of him.

The initiation into adulthood was not a one-off 'weekend special'. It could involve months of teaching about how to behave as a man, what responsibilities men took on, and where to find strength and direction. The ceremonies we normally hear about were only the marker events. Sometimes

BEWARE OF GOOD LOOKIN' SHEILAS –
DON'T OVERTIGHTEN WITH THAT WRENCH
– BUY LAND, SON – THEY'RE NOT
MAKING ANY MORE, HEH, HEH, HEH.

these ceremonies were harsh and frightening (and we would not want to return to these) but they were done with purpose and care, and were spoken of with great appreciation by those who had passed through them.

Traditional societies depended for their survival on raising competent and responsible young men. It was a life-and-death issue, never left to chance. They developed very proactive programmes for doing this, and the process involved the whole adult community in a concerted effort. (Some innovative ways we might go about this, appropriate to our times, are described in the final chapter, 'A Community Challenge'.)

In the Modern World

Mentoring today is mostly unplanned and piecemeal, and lots of young men don't receive any mentoring at all. Those doing the mentoring – sports coaches, uncles, teachers and bosses – rarely understand their role, and may do it badly. Mentoring used to happen in the workplace, especially under the apprenticeship system, whereby a young man learnt a great deal about attitudes and responsibilities along with his trade skills. This has all but disappeared – you won't get much mentoring while stacking shelves at the local supermarket.

Enlisting the Help of Others

The years from fourteen until the early twenties are for moving into the adult world, for separating from parents. Parents carefully and watchfully ease back. This is the time when a son develops a life which is quite separate from the family. He has teachers you barely know, experiences you never hear about, and he faces challenges that you cannot help him with. Pretty scary stuff.

A fourteen- or sixteen-year-old is far from ready to just be 'out there'. There have to be others to act as a bridge, and this is what mentors do. We should not leave youngsters in a peer group at this age without adult care. But a mentor is more than a teacher or a coach: a mentor is special to the child and the child is special to

him. A sixteen-year-old will not always listen to his parents – his inclination is not to. But a mentor is different. This is the time for the youngster to make his 'glorious mistakes', and part of the mentor's job is to make sure the mistakes are not fatal.

Parents have to ensure that mentoring happens – and they should have a big hand in choosing who does it. It really helps to belong to a strong social group – an active church, a family-minded sports club,

WHERE ARE YOU GOING?

YOUR PLACE!

a community-oriented school, or a group of friends who really care about each other.

You need to have these kinds of friends to provide what uncles and aunts used to – someone who cares about and enjoys your kids. These friends can show an interest in your youngsters, and ask them about their views. Hopefully they will make your kids welcome in their homes, 'kick their bum' occasionally, and be a listening ear when things at home are a little tense. (Many a mother has experienced a big fight with her teenage daughter, who then runs off to tell her woes to her mum's best friend down the road. This is what friends are for!)

You can do the same for their kids, too. Teenagers are quite enjoyable when they are not your own!

What If There Is No Mentor Available?

If there are no mentors around, then a young man will fall into a lot of potholes on the road to adulthood. He may fight needlessly with his parents in trying to establish himself as independent. He may just become withdrawn and depressed. Kids at this age have so many dilemmas and decisions – about sexuality, career choices, what to do about drugs and alcohol. If Mum and Dad keep spending time with him, and are in touch with his world, then he will keep talking to them about these things. But sometimes there will be a need to talk to other adults, too. In one study, it was shown that just one good adult friend outside the family was a significant preventative of juvenile crime (as long as the friend isn't *into* crime!).[11]

Young men will try their best to find structure and direction in their lives. They may choose born-again religion or an Eastern cult, disappear into the internet, follow Emo or Goth music and fashion, play sport, join a gang or go surfing. These pursuits may be helpful or harmful. If we don't have a community for kids to belong to, they will make their own. But a community made up only of the peer group is not enough – it may be just a group of lost souls, without the skills or knowledge to help each other. Many boys' friendship circles are really just loose collections that offer very little sharing or emotional support.

The worst thing we can do with adolescents is leave them alone. This is why we need those really great schoolteachers, sport coaches, scout leaders, youth workers and many other sources of adult involvement at this age. We need enough so that there is someone special for every kid – a tall order. Today we mostly get mothering right, and fathering is undergoing a great resurgence. Finding good mentors for the kids in our community is the next big hurdle.

STORIES FROM THE HEART

A LAKOTA INITIATION

The Native American people known as the Lakota were a vigorous and successful society, characterised by especially equal relationships between men and women.

At around the age of fourteen, Lakota boys were sent on a 'vision quest', or initiation test. This involved sitting and fasting on a mountain peak to await a vision or hallucination brought on by hunger. This vision would include a being who would bring messages from the spirit world to guide the boy's life. As the boy sat alone on the peak, he would hear mountain lions snarl and move in the darkness below him. In fact the sounds were made by the men of the tribe, keeping watch to ensure the boy's safety. A young person was too precious to the Lakota to endanger needlessly.

Eventually, when the young man returned to the tribe, his achievement was celebrated. But from that day, for two whole years, he was not permitted to speak directly to his mother.

Lakota mothers, like the women of all hunter-gatherer groups, are very close and affectionate with their children, and the children often sleep alongside them in the women's huts and tents. The Lakota believed that if the boy spoke to his mother immediately following his entry into manhood, the pull back into boyhood would be so great that he would 'fall' back into the world of childhood and never grow up.

After the two years had passed, a ceremonial rejoining of the mother and son took place, but by this time he was a man and able to relate to her as such. The reward that Lakota mothers gained from this 'letting go' is that they were assured their sons would return as respectful and close adult friends.

STORIES FROM THE HEART

THE STORY OF NAT, STAN AND THE MOTORBIKE

Nat was fifteen, and his life was not going well. He had always hated school and found writing difficult, and things were just mounting up. The school he went to was a caring school, and his parents, the counsellor and the principal knew each other and could talk comfortably. They met and decided that if Nat could find a job, they would arrange an exemption. Perhaps he was one of those boys who would be happier in the adult world than the in-between world of high school.

Luckily Nat got a job in a one-man pizza shop, Stan's Pizza, and left school. Stan, who was about thirty-five, was doing a good trade and needed help. Nat went to work there and loved it: his voice deepened, he stood taller, his bank balance grew. His parents, though, began to worry for a new reason. Nat planned to buy a motorbike – a *big* bike – to get to work. Their home was up a winding, slippery road in the mountains. They watched in horror as his savings got closer to the price of the motorcycle. They suggested a car, to no avail. Time passed.

One day Nat came home and, in the way of teenage boys, muttered something sideways as he walked past the dinner table. Something about a car. They asked him to repeat it, not sure if they should. 'Oh, I'm not going to get a bike. I was talking to Stan. Stan reckons a bloke'd be an idiot to buy a motorbike living up here. He reckons I should wait an' get a car.'

'Thank God for Stan!' thought his parents, but outwardly they just smiled and went on eating their meal.

PRACTICAL HELP

BOYS AND HEARING

Colin is ten. He is in trouble at school because he doesn't pay attention. He gets bored, starts to mess around, and gets sent to the principal's office. Is he stupid? Bad? Does he have ADHD or ODD (Oppositional Defiant Disorder) or OCD (Obsessive-Compulsive Disorder) or any of the other Ds? Perhaps, but there's another possibility. *What if he just can't hear?* What if his teacher's voice is too soft and he gets bored with its faintness, and at home he misses half of what is being said to him? Many parents joke that their son seems deaf when told to clean up his room. And school nurses have long noted that boys get blocked ears more frequently than girls. But there may be more serious factors at play.

Psychologist Leonard Sax, in his book, *Why Gender Matters*,[12] makes some extreme claims about boys' hearing. He presents research to show that boys do not hear as well as girls, and argues that boys need teachers who speak louder. He cites Janel Caine, a postgraduate student in Florida, who studied the effects of music on premature babies.[13] These babies lie in their incubators all day, and Caine felt that perhaps some gentle music might help their growth and development. And

boy, was she was right! In her astonishing findings, girl babies receiving music 'therapy' were discharged from the hospital on average nine days sooner than those who didn't have the music. It really perked them up! But here's the thing: boy babies did not show any such benefit. They either didn't hear the music, or it didn't affect them.

It's actually hard to know what tiny babies hear – we can't just ask them, 'Did you hear that?' But lately, some methods have been discovered that can tell if the brain is receiving the message that goes into the ears. Dr Sax claims that, in studies of 'acoustic brain response', girl babies have an 80 per cent greater brain response to sounds than baby boys do. And guess what frequency this is in? The frequency of speech.

The difference continues into adolescence and adulthood. This might explain that terrible syndrome – complained about by teenage girls worldwide – that Dad is always yelling at them, when Dad thinks he is using a gentle voice!

In a number of recent commentaries, however, Dr Sax has been accused of exaggerating or misrepresenting the research.[14] And it does stand to reason that if a huge gender hearing difference was the norm, audiologists would have told us about it earlier.

Nonetheless, there is no harm in being more hearing-aware around boys. And dads, if your daughters wince when you talk to them, maybe talk a little softer.

It's more likely that the problem of boys in school is not so much to do with hearing as with understanding. Australian audiologists Jan Pollard and Dr Kathy Rowe found that about a quarter of children aged six have poor auditory processing (separating what they hear into meaningful words). And most of these children (70 per cent) turn out to be boys. These children have trouble understanding a sentence if it has more than eight words in it! Because teachers often use much longer sentences when teaching, these kids are stuck trying to understand the first part while the teacher (or parent) is going full-steam ahead with the rest of the message. The researchers recommend that teachers use short sentences, and only go on speaking when they see that 'lights-on' effect in children's eyes.[15] And Dr Sax adds that perhaps boys should sit at the front of the class, not the back.

OVERCOMING BOYS' TENDENCY TO ARROGANCE

It's possible that boys are naturally prone to a certain degree of arrogance. Until recently, boys were often raised expecting to be waited on by women. In some cultures, boys are still treated like little gods. In today's world, the result can be an obnoxious boy that no one wants to be around.

It's therefore very important that boys are taught humility – through experiences such as having to apologise, having to do work to help others, and always having to be respectful to others. Kids have to know their place in the world, or the world will most likely teach them a harsh lesson.

Whenever you are treated badly by youngsters – jostled in the street by a skateboarder, treated rudely by a young salesperson, or have your house burgled – you are dealing with youngsters who have not been helped to fit in and be useful.

Teenagers are naturally prone to be somewhat self-absorbed, to fit their morality to their own self-interest, and to be thoughtless of others. Our job as parents is to engage them in vigorous discussions about their obligations to others, fairness, and plain right and wrong. We must reinforce some basics – 'Be responsible. Think things through. Consider others. Think of consequences'. Just loving your kids isn't enough, some toughness is necessary. Mothers begin this, fathers reinforce it, and elders add their weight if it still hasn't sunk in.

One good strategy is to have boys involved in service to others – the elderly, disabled people, or young children whom they help or teach. They learn the satisfaction of service, and they grow in self-worth at the same time.

IN A NUTSHELL

- In the years between birth and six, boys need lots of
  affection so they can 'learn to love'. Talking and teaching
  one-to-one helps them connect to the world. The mother is
  usually the best person to provide this, although a father can
  take this part.
- At about the age of six, boys show a strong interest in
  maleness, and the father becomes the primary parent. His
  interest and time become critical. The mother's part remains
  important, however: she shouldn't 'back off' from her son
  just because he is older.
- From about fourteen years of age, boys need mentors –
  other adults who care about them personally and who help
  them move gradually into the larger world. Old societies
  provided initiation to mark this stage, and mentors were
  much more available.
- Single mothers can raise boys well, but must search carefully
  for good, safe, male role models and must devote some time
  to self-care (since they are doing the work of two).

Chapter 3

Testosterone

Janine is pregnant – seven weeks pregnant – and very excited. She doesn't know it yet, but her baby is going to be a boy. We say 'going to be' because a foetus doesn't start that way.[1] It may surprise you to know that all young creatures start life being female. Boys are mutated girls! The Y chromosome that makes a baby into a boy is an 'add-on' chromosome which starts to act in the womb – to give a boy the extra bits he needs to be a boy and to stop other bits growing. A male is a female with optional extras. That's why everyone has nipples, though not everyone needs them.

Boys and Hormones

In Janine's baby's tiny body, at around the eighth week of pregnancy, the Y chromosomes stir in the cells and testosterone starts being made. As a result of this new chemical presence, the baby starts to become more of a boy, growing testicles and a penis and making other more subtle changes in his brain and body. Once the testicles are formed (by the fifteenth week), they start to make testosterone too, so he becomes progressively more and more masculine.

If Janine is *very* stressed, her body may suppress the testosterone in baby Jamie's body and he may not fully develop his penis and testicles, so he will be incompletely developed at birth. He will catch up, however, in the first year.

Right after birth, young Jamie will have as much testosterone in his bloodstream as a twelve-year-old boy! He has needed all this testosterone to stimulate his body to develop male qualities in time to be born. This 'testosterone hangover' will result in him having little erections from time to time as a newborn.

By three months of age, the testosterone level will drop off to about a fifth of the birth level, and throughout toddlerhood the level will stay pretty low. Boy and girl toddlers (I'm sure you'd agree) behave pretty much the same.

But the effects will now have set in motion a very different trajectory of brain development that will affect Jamie until his mid-twenties at least.[2] The biggest change will be a slowing of his brain growth, relative to his sisters at the same age. It will make him more vulnerable in certain ways that as parents we need to know about.

In 2017, a researcher called Alan Schore released a wide-ranging review of what we know about boys' neurological and emotional development.[3] Schore is held in awe by most of the child development world. He literally wrote the book on how we develop emotional wellbeing and how the brain and environment interact on a detailed, neurological level to create good mental health. His two massive tomes on the subject were the inspiration behind popular works such as Sue Gerhardt's ground-breaking *Why Love Matters*.[4] And his new message is that we need to worry about boys much more. The testosterone effects in the womb and the first year of life slow their brain development (especially in the right hemi-

sphere) so much that they are far more vulnerable than girls to anything that goes wrong. It sets boys up for mental health and behaviour problems much later if we don't maximise calm, responsive, and stress-free environments for them. He included the risk of endocrine disruptors[5] such as BPA in our water and food supply in pregnancy, a real concern about the use of daycare in the under-ones and the risks when parents are suffering violence, stress, mental illness, addictions or financial insecurity.

Schore points out that boys are so far behind girls in their brain development that 'the frontal cortex, caudate, and temporal lobes (the thoughtful and analytical parts of the brain) are faster growing in girls by as much as 20 months'. And 'at ages seven to 12 boys lag behind girls by as much as two years in social sensitivity'.[6] That's a heck of a delay, and means we really have to work on boys' abilities to think through their actions, understand their feelings and those of others, and be soothed and calmed by loving affection when they are upset. And we have to not blame or shame them for not being on the same trajectory as the girls they grow up alongside. The idea of boys as rough, tough and unemotional is completely wrong. They are full of feelings, they care deeply, and they need our help to get along with others. It's rather scary, but also hopeful – if we get this right, then the shut-down, messed-up men of today might one day be a thing of the past.

The Full-On Fours

Boys don't just develop at a different rate to girls. They also have unique developmental stages, triggered by hormonal shifts, which are only just being understood. The full-on fours is the first of these.

At around this age, millions of parents around the world notice their boys becoming more energetic, boisterous, and hard to keep quiet. It's not every boy, and some girls do this too, but it's a very common and a rather challenging thing. For centuries the answer to this abundance of boy energy was a pretty terrible one. Parents would yell at boys or hit them to make them quieten down. In schools canings and other cruelties were visited on generations of youngsters (including some girls) who could just not bear to be stuck at a desk, who fidgeted or were slow to learn their 3 Rs. A good child was one who stayed quiet and still, and so boys – most of them – were bad.

Then we began to think more deeply and with a bit more compassion about what we were expecting of boys. And some science came along that appeared to help. In the 1990s Professor Mitchell Harman at the US Department of Aging described a doubling in testosterone from around 40 ng/ml to around 80 ng/ml at this very age. It was a small, and brief rise (especially when compared with the almost tenfold rise that drives puberty in the early–mid teens). I reported this as a possible explanation of the changed behaviour. Many people found this a helpful piece of information, and all over the world people became more understanding of their boys and gave them more scope to be physically active, and were more empathic while helping them learn to get along. Schools and childcare centres took steps to ensure that boys were not cooped up for too long, and built more chances for movement and activity into their day.

It was never an excuse for misbehaviour, but a message that we needed to help boys find ways to be *safely* active and physical. Occupational therapists added their input that at four boys are still developing their gross motor brain–muscle wiring, and so it's more than just letting off steam. Movement is something all children need to grow their brains, but for boys that stage lasts longer.

However there was one problem – in the years that followed, the findings described by Professor Harman were not corroborated, and other endocrinologists doubted them. In fact, it was still an area that received very little study – the only study I could find began at age six, missing the four-year-old phase entirely. In subsequent editions I reported that this was a controversial finding that we could not rely on. Then some more information came to light. As is often the case with hormones, it turned out to be more complicated. What *does* happen at four is that boys' bodies start to release luteinising hormone which tells their testes to start making Leydig cells, which are the little factories for testosterone which will ramp up in puberty. Luteinising hormone levels in four-year-old boys pulsate every day in exactly the way that testosterone levels do in adults, though we do not know why.[7] So in a sense, four is the start of the puberty process. Whether this directly or indirectly causes the behaviour changes we have no idea.

In 2017, Professor Kate Steinbeck, a specialist in children's endocrinology at the University of Sydney, offered her explanation of the 'full-on fours' stage:

So, is there an alternative explanation for boys' behaviour at this age, which parents regularly report?

1. We see differences in boys' and girls' brains and behaviour well before puberty. Rises in testosterone in the womb and during the mini-puberty in the first six months of life likely explain these.
2. Studies that look at behaviour in four- to five-year-olds … show boys and girls this age generally have different ways of playing and communicating. Boys' play is generally more physical. Girls generally have more socially interactive play, and are more articulate.
3. Interestingly, girls with congenital adrenal hyperplasia, who are exposed to high levels of testosterone in the womb, tend to have more 'rough and tumble' play styles, consistent with a testosterone effect on early brain development.

So, how might being four or five change boys' behaviour?

At this age, children learn how to interact with others, understand another's needs, share, and to deal with new and unfamiliar situations. Boys may respond more physically and be less able to articulate what happened. Learning how to regulate their emotions is an important skill for children to develop. Parents can model good emotional regulation, make sure children have regular daily routines, enough time to practice play and enough sleep. Praising positive behaviour and not overreacting to minor attention-seeking misbehaviour also helps.

Persistent and distressing behaviours in a child may signal underlying anxieties, reaction to family stresses, or be a result of adversities when they were younger. So, if you are concerned, seek professional advice.

For all children, we need to prioritise time to play. That could mean space, action and permission to be noisy and boisterous.[8]

So, in other words, it *is* testosterone, but the causes are earlier in life, only coming to the fore through the stresses of being four!

There is something we need to remember here. For 99 per cent of human history, we were a very physical and lively species – we moved about all the time. In hunter-gatherer society, four-year-old boys are just leaving toddlerhood, and start rapidly acquiring the stamina, strength, and amazing physical dexterity needed for their adult lives. (I lived with and studied hunter-gatherer people in the mountains of West New Britain in the 1970s, and from the very first day I was astonished at how capable and independent small children were, often accompanying us on long journeys without any sign of fatigue. Nothing saddens me more than seeing the cooped-up tiny spaces that urban children now live in, or the way our schooling forces kids to stay sitting for long periods in the same place.)

At four, boys start onto their real boyhood, and for many of them that includes a great need for movement and action. It's a serious parental challenge to find ways for our boys (and girls) to express their physical energy safely and sociably, and still stay connected to them and their feelings so they know they are loved. In fact, the whole challenge of being male, lifelong, is learning that it's possible

to be energetic and safe, boisterous and thoughtful, adventurous and responsible. Understanding your boy's nature is the first step. The second step is engaging with him and helping him to learn how to steer it well. That takes patience, empathy, and good-humoured persistence. The whole purpose of this book is to help you with that.

STORIES FROM THE HEART

A PARENT'S POINT OF VIEW

One anonymous parent on a discussion forum put it better than I ever could have, so I am going to let her have the last word:

> I think if you ask a lot of parents with both girls and boys they will confirm that this effect with boys seems to be a real thing. It happens in home-educated kids as much as ones in school/ nursery at this age. It also happens in families like mine where we made a real, informed effort not to introduce gender stereotypes (I mean, I lived in a radical feminist commune for five years). My experience is that yes, there is a push for independence at age four to five … but it's more an aggression, a wild energy, an inability to listen to instructions. I actually think almost every single neurotypical boy I know has hit this … and it often leaves parents reeling and gets labelled as bad behaviour. I don't much think it matters what causes it, personally, whether it's social or chemical. And I am completely up for the idea that some girls will also experience something like this, though I saw nothing like what I saw in my son in my two girls. I think sometimes people see it as an excuse for bad behaviour in boys and it's not. What I think is important is that it is a real phenomenon and needs to be treated as such, and that is far more important to me than the biochemistry behind it.

By six, young Jamie is out of the changes we have described, and seems to settle down. He can handle school better, and focus more. He still loves to be active, but is more sociable. He is not terribly interested in girls, but gets along well if they share interests. You can breathe a sigh of relief. Enjoy these years of respite, because you have earned them. And because, just round the corner are the 'insecure eights'!

Adrenarche – the Eight-Year-Old Meltdown and What to Do About It

After a few easy years, Jamie's parents notice something odd. Once a calm and contented boy, at around eight years of age (or it may be a little later in some boys), he may start being more emotional and easily upset. What does this mean? Some remarkable new findings have been made about a stage at least two years before puberty, that affects the emotional stability of boys.[9] If you have an eight-year-old who has become much more tearful or bad-tempered around the age of eight, this may be what is going on. (Of course, you should also check out other possible causes – that something bad hasn't happened to him – just to be on the safe side.)

In a long-term study of 1,200 boys at Melbourne's Murdoch Institute, it was discovered that adrenarche makes boys have greater emotional problems at this age.[10] (In girls, that did not happen until real puberty came along.)

Puberty in boys, which has obvious signs like pubic hair, deepening voice, and so on, usually happens at around ten to thirteen years of age. But adrenarche comes a couple of years sooner, and is the preparatory, and largely invisible, stage as a boy's body gets ready for the leap into manhood. While there are few outer changes, on the inside things are bubbling up. It's not that young Jamie is actually feeling angry, but he is just more easily rattled or upset (though of course it can turn into aggression in an insecure boy or one who sees lots of violence around him). And so Jamie's parents may need to be more understanding, and helpful as he navigates feelings he isn't used to.

Here is how one mother described it.

Our son had always been good-natured and gentle but when he was in Grade 4 (eight to nine years old) he would get so angry and frustrated at things that never used to bother him before. We've always been able to talk about these things and so luckily he could tell us: 'sometimes I get so angry I just want to hit something', for example, after a little tiff with his younger sister, who knew how to push his buttons. In the past he had been able to shrug that off. Now, you could see the anger rising in him and that he was scared and didn't like feeling this way. We gave him some tools to help cope, like going into his room and hitting his pillow if he had to (to avoid him hitting his sister, which he never did, by the way). We also contacted his primary school and asked the counsellor to have a chat with him. The counsellor was great, and reiterated the things we were telling him: go for a walk, distract your mind, etc., but coming from someone with authority it backed up our parenting and gave him another outlet if he needed it. Things started to settle down after about twelve months. We still have our gentle caring young man and I put it down to pre-pubescent hormones starting to 'kick in'. He's now fourteen and going great.

(Our thanks to Burnice B. for this great description.)

What to Do

1. Be understanding. If he has a meltdown during the day, choose a time to discuss it, for example at bedtime, when he will feel calmer and more able to talk.
2. Talk to him about how he is feeling, and ask what it is like for him when those emotions come up. Getting it into words always helps.

3. Explain to him about the changes of adrenarche when his body is getting ready for puberty in a year or two's time, and how his hormones stir up emotions more strongly than in the past.
4. Explain that it will settle down. And his feelings still matter, they have a purpose, and that you can work with him to make life more easy, when he experiences things like unfairness, aggression or thoughtlessness in others. He isn't imagining things, just reacting more strongly than usual.
5. Strategies like going for a walk to cool off, doing some exercise to let off steam, or talking to you about it, are all fine.

Somewhere between the ages of ten and thirteen, puberty proper finally sets in. Testosterone levels start to rise steadily. Eventually – usually around fourteen – they will increase by some 800 per cent over the level of toddlerhood. (When I mention this in my talks on *Raising Boys*, I pause as a ripple of fright runs across the auditorium like a Mexican wave!) The passage to manhood has now begun. There is no need to be afraid – adolescence is often given a bad rap, whereas it is really an exciting and heart-warming time, though of course it has its challenges. Once again, it's all about being prepared.

Brains Go Out of the Window

Jamie's adolescence can't be missed. It starts with a sudden growth and elongation of his arms and legs – so much so that his whole nervous system has to rewire itself. He gets clumsy and awkward. On the inside, neural pruning is massive as his brain starts to reshape into the much more focused mind needed for adulthood. In about 50 per cent of boys, testosterone levels are so high that some of it converts into oestrogen, and breast swelling and tenderness may be experienced. This is nothing to worry about.

By thirteen, the reorganisation of Jamie's brain makes him dopey and disorganised for many months. His mother and father have to act as his substitute brain for a while! If they're not aware of the reasons for this, parents can wonder where they have gone wrong.

But if Jamie's parents know this is all part of puberty, and take a relaxed – if vigilant – attitude, then things should work out just fine.

By fourteen, the testosterone level is now at a peak, and pubic hair, acne, strong sexual feelings and a general restlessness may well drive Jamie and everyone around him slightly crazy. For most families this is the most challenging year of raising boys – take comfort

that if you hang in and stay caring and firm, it does pass. The later teens find boys getting increasingly more sensible and mature.

Eventually, when Jamie reaches his mid-twenties, things will settle down, hormonally speaking. His testosterone levels are just as high, but his body has become used to them. His erections are a little more under control! The hormone continues to endow him with male features – high cholesterol, baldness, hairy nostrils and so on – well into later life. On the plus side, the testosterone gives him surges of creative energy, a love of competition, and a desire to achieve and to be protective. Hopefully his energies will be channelled into activities and career choices (as well as a happy sex life) which bring all kinds of satisfaction and benefits.

In his early forties, Jamie's levels of testosterone will begin a very gradual decline. He goes for several days at a time without thinking about sex! In the bedroom, quality replaces quantity. In the big world, Jamie now has less to prove, and is more mellow and wise. He assumes quiet leadership in group and work situations, rather than having to prove who's boss. He values friendship and makes his best contributions to the world.

Each Boy Is Different

What we have described here is the pattern for the average boy. There is great variation among males and also lots of overlap between the sexes. Some girls will have more testosterone-type behaviour than some boys, and some boys will show more oestrogen-type behaviour than some girls. Nonetheless, the general pattern will hold true for most children.

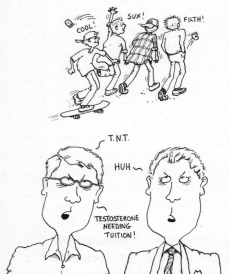

Understanding boys' hormones and their effects means we can understand what is going on and be sympathetic and helpful. Just as a good husband understands his partner's PMT (premenstrual tension), a good parent of a boy understands his TNT (testosterone needing tuition).

Why Boys Scuffle and Fight

Testosterone affects mood and energy levels; it's more than just a growth hormone. That's why, for centuries, horses were gelded to make them better behaved. (I know, don't go there!) Testosterone injected into female rats makes them try to mate with other female rats and fight with each other. It makes certain parts of the brain grow and others slow down their growth. It can grow more muscles and less fat, and it can make you go bald and bad-tempered!

How testosterone affects the psychology of males can be illustrated by a famous study. A tribe of monkeys in a laboratory was closely observed to learn about its social structure. Researchers found that the male monkeys had a definite hierarchy, or pecking

PRACTICAL HELP

TEENAGE BOYS AND CARS

The biggest single worry for most parents of boys is safety. In the adolescent years, as he spends more time away from your direct care and his mobility and independence grow, it's hard to relax and just 'let go'. And in fact there is growing evidence that this fear is well grounded, that we are letting go too soon. This is especially true in the matter of driving cars. Every year the newspapers carry stories of small towns or suburban communities across the nation devastated by multiple fatality crashes, where four or five teenagers die in collisions caused by immaturity and inexperience.

As a community we care deeply about the lives of our young people, and this has prompted some astounding research into why boys die like this and how to prevent it. It has been discovered that one boy on his own driving a car, aged in his late teens, is relatively safe. Today's emphasis on driver training and 50–100 hours of practise driving with an adult supervising (usually Mum or Dad) means young men have greater awareness and skill than young drivers in our day. They probably drive too fast at times, but are also more focused on and attentive to their driving, so they do not fare too badly as long as alcohol is not involved. However, if you add a male passenger in the car, things begin to change: the young driver takes more risks, and the chances of a fatal crash increase by 50 per cent. If the passenger is a girl, however, a male driver usually becomes protective and careful, and is actually safer than he is on his own.

The next part will shock you. If you now add one or more other young people in the back seat, the death rate of the driver increases by over 400 per cent. The distraction, the need to impress, and the diffi-culty of staying in a calm, careful state of mind, mean that all those in the car are at serious risk. This is especially so after dark, and of course is much worse with drugs or alcohol present.[11] This astonishingly clear research has lead to law reforms that are saving lives around the world.

In Australia, a bereaved father, Rob Wells, who lost his son along with three other boys in a single car crash, has campaigned to persuade governments in several states to restrict young drivers carrying more than one passenger, especially late at night. These laws have worked very effectively in New Zealand and Canada for many years.

Meanwhile, it helps that parents know about this 'brain overload factor' – the 'maturity bypass effect' of having friends in a car – and can make informed decisions. Psychologists now believe seventeen-year-olds are too young to drive groups of friends about at any time. You have ferried them about for sixteen years already; why not do it for another year or two, to know they won't die or kill their friends?

At seventeen, teenagers can sound persuasive. They can say the right things. But it's later, under pressure, that their brains are not able to cope. The last thing parents of dead teenagers ever hear them say is, 'I'll be fine, Mum'. A year or two later, and with more experience, they will be so much safer.

order. The females' hierarchy was looser and more relaxed, based on who groomed whose hair! But the males always knew who was boss, sub-boss, and sub-sub-boss, and had frequent fights to prove it.[12]

Once the researchers had worked out the monkey dynamics, they set about stirring up trouble. They captured the lowest-ranking male monkey and gave him an injection of testosterone. Then they put him back with the tribe. You can guess what happened next. He started a boxing match with his 'immediate superior'. Much to his own surprise, he won! So he went and took on the next monkey. Our hero was small, but he had testosterone. He became the 'acting manager'.

Sadly for him, this was not to last. The injection soon wore off, and our little hero was knocked back all the way down to the bottom of the heap. It's a lot like politics!

Boys Need Order

In their book, *Raising a Son*,[13] Don and Jeanne Elium tell the story of an old scoutmaster who comes and sorts out a hopelessly rowdy scout troop in their city. This is the 'scout troop from hell': the boys are always fighting and damaging the hall, nothing is being learnt, and many gentler boys have left. It's time for a clean sweep. On his first night with the troop, the scoutmaster sets some rules, invites a couple of boys to shape up or leave, brings in a clear structure, and begins teaching skills in an organised way. He successfully turns the group around: in a couple of months it is thriving.

The scoutmaster explained to the Eliums that, in his experience, there are three things boys always need to know:

1. Who's in charge?
2. What are the rules?
3. Will those rules be fairly applied?

The Key Word Is Structure

Boys feel insecure and in danger if there isn't enough structure in a situation. If no one is in charge, they begin jostling with each other to establish a pecking order. Their make-up leads them to want to set up hierarchies, but they can't always do so because they are all the same age. If we provide structure, then they can relax. For girls, this is not so much of a problem.

Many years ago I spent time in the slums of Calcutta to learn about families there. At first glance, Calcutta seemed chaotic and frightening. In fact, though, there were ganglords and neighbourhood hierarchies – and these, for better or worse, provided a structure for people to live their lives. You were safer with a structure – even a mafia-like structure – than with none. As a better structure was provided by religious or community leaders who were trustworthy and competent, life improved. Wherever you see a gang of boys looking unruly, you know the adult leadership is failing. Boys form gangs for survival – it's their attempt to have a sense of belonging, order and safety.

Boys act tough to cover up their fear. If someone is clearly the boss, they relax. But the boss must not be erratic or punitive. If the person in charge is a bully, the boys' stress levels rise and it's back to the law of the jungle. If the teacher, scoutmaster or parent is kind and fair (as well as being strict), then boys will drop their 'macho' act and get on with learning.

This seems to be an in-built gender difference. If girls are anxious in a group setting they tend to be quiet, whereas boys respond by running about and making a lot of noise. This has been mistakenly seen as boys 'dominating the space' but it is actually an anxiety response. Schools which are very good at engaging boys in interesting and concrete activities (such as Montessori schools, where there is a lot of structural work with blocks, shapes, beads and so on) greatly reduce this gender difference in children's behaviour.[14]

Not everyone accepts that hormones affect boys' behaviour. Some feminists have argued that men have testosterone through conditioning – that it comes from being raised that way. There is actually a partial truth in this: one study found that boys in scary or violent school environments produced more testosterone.[15] When the same school introduced a more supportive environment – where teachers did not abuse or threaten, where bullying was tackled with special programmes – the boys' levels of testosterone dropped measurably. So environment *and* biology both play a part. Environment *influences* the hormone. Nature – and boys' inbuilt calendar – creates it. Success with boys means accepting their nature while directing it in good ways. If you know what you are dealing with, it's a whole lot easier and you don't need to blame anyone – just help them find a better way.

Guiding the 'High–drive' Boys

Studies into hormone levels in the womb (studied by sampling the umbilical cord at birth) show that there are big variations in testosterone levels among individual boys. There are high-T and low-T boys and this affects their nature too.

Early in the school year, teachers often notice a certain kind of boy who will either become a hero of the class or a complete villain. For this boy there is no middle ground. This type of boy stands out by his:

- challenging behaviour and competitiveness
- greater physical maturity, and
- high energy levels.

If the teacher is able to engage such a boy and direct his energies in good ways, the boy will thrive and be a plus in the school. If the teacher or parent ignores, backs off or is negative towards the boy, then the boy's pride will depend on defeating the adult, and problems will compound. These boys have leadership potential, but leadership has to be taught from an early age.

The final message of all this is that even on a chemical level, every boys is unique. But there are forces that shape him. You have to continually get to know him, and his changes, and love him regardless, but always be active, and sometimes forceful, in helping him keep a warm heart, and grow a strong backbone. The coming chapters will talk much more about how.

IN A NUTSHELL

- Hormones in varying degrees affect every boy. They give him growth spurts, make him want to be active, and make him competitive and in need of strong guidelines and a safe, ordered environment.
- They trigger significant changes, some immediate and some delayed:
  - at four – into activity and boyishness
  - at thirteen – into rapid growth and disorientation, and
  - at fourteen – into testing limits and breaking through to early manhood.
- The boy with lots of testosterone needs special help to develop leadership qualities and to channel his energies in good ways.
- A boy needs to learn empathy and feeling, and be shown tenderness if he is to be a caring person.
- Some girls have a lot of testosterone but, on the whole, it's a boy thing – and it needs our understanding, not blame or ridicule. Testosterone equals vitality, and it's our job to steer it in healthy directions.

Chapter 4

Making a New Kind of Man

It's clear we need a different kind of man to those the twentieth century often created. We want them to have open hearts, and be able to step out of that old toxic masculinity that was shut down, harsh and cold. The suicide rates and depression that plague men are one reason we have to change this. The intractable problems of family violence are another. And then there's the state of the world! The incredible, exciting thing is that we know how to do this.

In this chapter we will look at three big life skills that boys today need, and how to pass them on to your son. The first is being able to respond comfortably to discipline or boundaries. The second is being able to express emotions, especially the vulnerable ones like fear or sadness, and still feel secure and OK. This includes the big one for all males – being able to cry. And finally, being able to use words to solve problems, think clearly and avoid doing dumb things from lack of thought. These are skills that can keep your son alive – they really are hugely important. So let's begin.

Discipline Without Stress

Danny, aged two, is a chubby-cheeked, laughing toddler, who loves his mum, and his teddy bear and his life. He is just finishing his dinner, and decides to stand up and climb over the back of his chair, which is precariously high off the ground. His mum tells him to sit back down. It's OK if he wants to get down and play, but he can't climb on his chair like that.

Danny keeps on climbing. A generation ago, most parents would have told him off, and possibly a big fight would ensue. Perhaps he would be smacked or sent to his room, and at least be yelled at or scolded. Or he would have been given in to and let go.

But Danny's mum doesn't do either. She speaks gently but clearly, 'you aren't allowed to climb on the chair like that' and as his face crumples, she goes closer to him and softly says, 'I know, it's hard when you can't do what you want' and gives him a hug, her face right against his. 'I wanna climb!' he sobs. 'I know, but you can't. It's OK! You can sit and talk to us, or get down and play. It's fine!'

Something interesting happens. Suddenly he is being intensely nurtured and he can't stay unhappy. You can actually see on his face the struggle fading away. He turns back to face the table where the others are still eating and stays put after all. People smile at him and include him in the conversation. It's important to note here, in case you missed it – he doesn't get his 'way'. But he is helped with being able to move past that.

What a new generation of parents seem to be learning is that you can do discipline without harshness or conflict or a battle of wills. That we do often have to thwart toddlers' plans, but that doesn't make them naughty, or us mean, and it can often be done without fighting. Being a toddler and pre-schooler is all about learning to get along with other people, and stay out of danger, and sometimes just not get what you want – and feel OK about it. This method treats everyday conflicts as a chance to go on learning that.

If we see our job as just keeping control of 'misbehaviour', then the risk is that we will be too cold and critical – making little boys (especially if they are very active and noisy) feel that they are bad. And most likely, rebellious and secretive. Or if we just give in, that they will remain the victim of their own impulses, not learn boundaries, and grow up with no ability to just drop something and walk away.

The idea of 'badness' in boys is deep in the culture. The childhood of Australia's most famous serial killer Ivan Milat provides a very vivid example. Milat's mother was allegedly once seen arguing with him in the playground after school. She became enraged at something he said, knocked him to the ground and began wildly kicking and stamping on him where he lay. He was about six at the time. His dad was also violent, possibly more so. It's not far-fetched to connect this childhood with the kind of man he became. Acutely anxious about maintaining control, many parents may resort to verbal and then physical violence. In much of the world this is still the primary parenting fall-back, and the result is generations of violent men.

That's why it's so important that we work with boys to show that we love them even as we set limits on their behaviour. And, of course, it's a lot easier if you start young. (Though you may, with an older boy, sit down and talk about how in the past you were more negative, and you want to change that. And if he wants that too, his part will be to calm down too, and think more and work with you to sort things out by talking.) Or, if you erred on the slack side and have been poor at setting boundaries, then you might want to sit them down and say, 'I think I have often confused you by being unclear about where the boundaries are in our family. I need to change that, so that you know what you can and can't do.'

The long-term goal is to teach a boy to simply let go. To drop what they wanted or were doing, when it isn't working for the people around them. Think how important that is going to be in school, and when they grow up, in their sex life, in the workplace. It doesn't make them a wimp, just not the prisoner of their ego or their impulses. It's the difference, in a sense, between a boy and a man.

The 'terrible twos' are terrible only when we don't know how to be warm-hearted about drawing boundaries with children. If we are gentle, understanding, and show empathy even as we tell them they can't do what they are doing (even at those times when we need to pick them up and carry them away), then they soon learn to calm their feelings at being thwarted. It might mean sitting with a child and cuddling them, even you have just stopped them in their tracks, to help them get over the feelings of upset they are having. Or if they are just furious, you can give them some space. But most often, they were needing that closeness, and their management of their own wild impulses will be improved without doing any harm to their spirit. There are plenty of other ways they can be happy and free, just not ones involving running with scissors, hitting their friends or falling from the back of their chair.

Boys and Crying

There has been no greater revolution in our ideas of manhood than the realisation that crying is good for you. That big men do cry. There is some powerful science to support this: when we have a loss, large or small, our brain is wounded, literally, because the neural connections are suddenly changed. What was there in our life is no longer there. It can be a favourite toy left behind on holiday, or a beloved grandparent who has died, a friend at school who moves away, or someone you trusted treating you meanly. Who can predict what in the mind of a child feels like a terrible loss? Our brains were designed for this because human life has always had intense grief as part of it. So we have evolved healing mechanisms. When human beings experience grief, their eyes run, and they sob, and their whole body shudders. In their bloodstream strong doses of endorphins are released and this helps the brain to start to heal up the 'tearing' of connections that now don't go where they used to. Neuroscientists only learnt about this when tears were analysed and found to contain the endorphins in very large amounts – because they were in all the body fluids at that time.

Crying is how we get over things, and there is no other way it can be done. We all have the ability to set aside our emotions, because they don't help in a crisis. A teary surgeon or soldier in a firefight can't even see straight, so we need the ability to put our feelings on hold. But if that crisis is long-lasting, such as being deployed for months and years in war zones, or having a dad who comes home drunk every night, or poverty and stress with no end, then sometimes we shut down our emotions so strongly that it's hard to find them when the danger is gone.

This happened to millions of men in the twentieth century, and most of those became dads. And so 'big boys don't cry' became the way we taught our sons. And it was just plain wrong. Big boys who don't cry generally use alcohol instead, hit people, implode, explode, get addicted to something or kill themselves. (Men kill themselves at about 20–30 times the rate that they kill other people.) Shutting off your feelings isolates you. But being vulnerable – in other words, showing your emotions – helps others feel close to you.

In this generation men have started learning to cry again, and it's a huge help. I've treated veterans from four wars, and men from countless disasters, and it's always a turning point when they are able to cry.[1]

Some Things You Can Do ...

- Never tell a boy to stop crying.
- Affirm them in words and action when they do cry, saying – as you hug them or stand close at their side – 'you've got such a good heart', 'you're a great kid, you really care' or 'it's really sad what's happened'.
- Cry yourself, when you need to, and don't apologise for it. Especially if you are a dad, this is wonderful. At the same time, if you have really strong grief that can make you look out of control or not secure in your own role as a parent, even momentarily, then keep those tears to a time when you are with another adult or on your own. There are emotions that kids can't deal with in those they are depending on. You can cry wholeheartedly alongside your children, but they need to know you are OK, and solid, even in the midst of that.
- Just say things matter-of-factly about sadness and crying. When watching television – 'that's really sad', 'Oh, that makes me so sad' – especially coming from a dad, is great permission that all emotions have their place. Likewise for fear – and happiness.

When boys can be as sad, scared, happy as they want, then the fourth feeling – anger – will be much less of a problem. It won't be substituted for the others and make a boy into a walking time-bomb. A boy who can cry finds peace and calm and connection to those who love him.

Talking, Reading, Thinking – How Words Can Save Your Son's Life

The moment that fourteen-year-old Marcus walks in from school, he can sense that there is something wrong. His mum looks upset, and she sits him down to tell him why. His dad, who does not live with them, had promised to spend the first week of the holidays taking Marcus on a fishing and camping trip. He has called a week ahead of the trip to say he can't make it. He phoned when Marcus was at school, probably because he didn't want to tell him himself.

Marcus's face clouds over. He blurts out 'It's OK, I don't mind', but then goes quickly from the room and won't talk about it any more. His mum knows that he is crushed, he had been talking about and planning the trip for weeks.

At school the next day, his drama teacher sees he is not his usual self. She waits until after class, and asks him if anything is wrong. He says 'no'. She doesn't believe him, but gives him a concerned look and lets it go.

On the Thursday night, Marcus doesn't come home from hanging with his friends at the shops. His mum can't get him to answer his phone. At 10.00 p.m. she goes out to look for him, and at 11.00 p.m. she calls the police.

Life gives most kids hard knocks sometimes, and they take it in different ways. Some are able to tell caring adults and friends about it, get a handle on things and express their hurts and disappointments, and get over it. But even today many boys will bottle things up. A trigger incident can turn into a disaster. What is the reason that Marcus has not come home? Perhaps he has stolen a car with friends, and crashed it? Perhaps he has been hurt or hurt someone else in a fight? Perhaps he has got blind drunk or taken drugs and is lying in an alley somewhere? Or perhaps he will just come home safe and sound, but still harbouring a big lake of negative feelings that might flood out another time? Celia Lashley, who ran a men's prison for many years, said most of the inmates were there because of five seconds of poor decision-making.[2]

At midnight, Marcus calls. He is very apologetic, explaining that he just needed to be alone, and went up into the hills. His mum calls the police and lets them know he is safe. They share a big hug when he arrives at the door, shivering and cold but otherwise fine.

How do we help our boys to stay safe and well? A surprising thing really helps – we have to help them to use words – language – to express and deal with their lives. It starts from babyhood in the way we talk and interact with them to help them say what they feel and need. So that when they are older, it comes naturally to talk. And to feel OK to be vulnerable and in touch with their emotions.

Marcus was deeply sad at his father's letting him down. It meant – to him – that he wasn't worth spending time with. But he did not experience it this way. He felt numb and compressed, and intensely pent up. The closest thing to an emotion he could allow was anger. Anger is a less vulnerable feeling than shame and disappointment.

Had he been able to talk about how let-down he felt, then he could have decompressed, and had more ability to be rational about what to do. He could have worked out that he was a worthwhile and great kid, whatever his father did or did not do. Using words to help us through vulnerable places, and to reason and make freer choices, is what makes us fully human.

Today everyone knows that it's important to read books to small children. But the real reason is more than you might think. By reading, kids learn that life can make sense. They learn the language by which they can think. That lives have stories, and we can choose a good or bad story for ourselves. That all behaviour has reasons, and there is an inner world of feelings which can be navigated safely. (You don't learn a lot about feelings by watching television because you only see the actions, not the reasons. And on television the language is dumbed down. 'Oh yeah?' 'I'll show you!')

There is another reason that this matters – most boys' brains are slower to acquire language skills, and need our help to be able to express things in words, as well as read and write fluently. And more importantly, to enjoy both of these things. In fact according to recent studies, the more testosterone a boy has (measured in his umbilical cord at birth) the slower his brain develops these skills.[3]

Reading to our boys – making it fun, close and special – hooks them on stories, and soon they are doing it for themselves. (Not having too much television, especially not having it in bedrooms, makes it more likely that boys will read more.)

Reading is just part of it. Talking to them, chatting to and fro, letting them answer, giving them time to think, choosing your time and place (like, in the car, where they are less self-conscious, or while doing some activity together) helps boys start to sort out their feelings, air their dilemmas and tell you their worries. And their dreams and hopes. Be careful not to swamp a boy with your words, or endless questions. Give them space and patient quiet attention as they find the words to say what they feel or mean. If you don't judge or get all overprotective, they will tell you more and more about their thoughts.

Other adults like uncles or aunts, grandmas or grandpas can sometimes do this really well. By showing they are interested, they let a boy know they are keeping an eye on him. That they expect updates, and that he can always go to their house and hang out or sleep over. That way he has a range of people in his life both accepting him, and expecting the best from him.

Men and boys weren't always so mute. In Shakespeare's day, it was ordinary street people who went to those intricate fast-moving plays at the Globe Theatre each night. Charles Dickens' books were printed in weekly serial form, and families read them at the dinner table. The language in those books is full of subtlety, but ordinary kids loved to hear them. We've got dumber in the way we talk, as well as how little we talk, or have time to talk, and our kids' lives and choices may be dumber as a result.

Reading, thinking and talking work together so a boy has a handle on life, a tool he can use to solve conflicts when he is grown up and in relationship, workplaces, and is a dad himself. We've had mute, messed-up boys and men for too long, and the world needs them to be open-hearted and able to express themselves. Words are how we think and connect, and that is what sets us free. And sometimes, what keeps us alive.

PRACTICAL HELP

HOW TO HAVE A TALK-ABLE BOY

Sadly, in every classroom, there are usually four or five children who can't read, write or speak well. And among these children, boys outnumber girls by four to one.[4] You can help your boy learn to communicate better, starting right from when he is a baby. Here's how.

1. 'TALK THEM UP' – ONE STEP AT A TIME

Children acquire spoken language one step at a time. Babies under one year of age will begin to babble and gesture very enthusiastically, telling us they are ready to learn verbal communication! This is the time to start to teach them words.

- When your baby starts to babble, repeat a word that seems to be what he means. Baby says 'gukuk, baguk!' and points to his toy duck. You say 'Ducky! Luke's ducky!' Soon Luke will be saying 'Ducky' too.

- With a toddler who says single words, like 'milk!', you say a couple of words back to them, such as 'milk bottle'. This helps him to move on to joining pairs of words together.
- A child who is saying words in twos and threes can be stretched further by imitating you in whole sentences. For example, he says, 'Gavin truck!' You reply, 'Gavin wants his truck? Here's Gavin's truck!' And so on. Do it with a spirit of excitement and fun, not earnest hard work.

In short, kids learn best if you speak back to them one step ahead of the stage they are at. And they love the game – all human beings love to communicate.

2. TAKE EVERY CHANCE YOU CAN TO EXPLAIN THINGS TO CHILDREN

This is a great use of the many times when you are just doing routine things with your children – travelling, doing housework, going for a walk, doing the shopping. Use this time to chatter, to point things out, and to answer questions. Surprisingly, some very loving parents (who care for their kids well) seem not to realise that kids' brains grow from conversation. Don't be shy – explain things, tell them stories! For example, 'You see this lever? This makes the wipers go. They swish the rain away from the window.' 'This vacuum cleaner makes a big wind. It sucks the air and pulls the dirt into a bag. Would you like a turn?'

This kind of talk – provided you don't overdo it and bore your child senseless – does more for your child's brain than any amount of expensive education later on.

3. READ TO YOUR KIDS FROM AN EARLY AGE

Even when your child is just one year old, you can enjoy books together – especially the kind that have rhymes and repetition. From enjoying them on your knee or snuggled up in bed, children learn to love books, looking at the pictures and enjoying the sound of your voice. You can ham it up a little by making funny voices or by being dramatic.

As your child gets to have favourite stories, you can play a 'predicting' game: 'And the little cat went …?', pausing so your child provides the 'Miaow!'. Prediction is a very important part of reading. Good readers anticipate what word is coming next.

Remember, whenever you're playing learning games with kids, the trick is to be playful, making your children 'stretch' their minds just a little – which they will love to do.

All kids benefit from these learning games – but for boys it is also a preventive step because of their disposition to be poorer at language if we don't help them along. And it's fun to do, anyway!

If you have worries about your boy's speech and language development (if he isn't talking as well as you think he should), trust your intuition. Speak to a speech therapist from your local hospital or community health centre. Sessions of speech therapy are fun for children and can make all the difference to a good start.

(Our thanks to Dr Jenny Harasty for these tips.)

IN A NUTSHELL

- We need a different, and better equipped, kind of man for the twenty-first century.
- If we help kids understand and deal with their emotions, we can do discipline without having it be a big conflict.
- Emotional openness, including being able to cry, is healthy for boys and men. Vulnerability is the key to good mental health, because without it we can't be close to others, or grow and learn.
- Being able to use words is essential to make sense of our lives, think through choices, and connect with each other. Talking and reading to boys really matters.

Chapter 5

What Dads Can Do

My daughter is now a young woman, yet it seems like only yester-day that she was being born. That was a day to remember! We had planned on a home birth, but had a back-up plan for a hospital transfer if necessary. And sure enough, the labour ended with an emergency Caesarean at about 3 a.m. – not at all what we had hoped for. The pact I'd made with my wife Shaaron was, 'nobody else takes this baby'. So I was there in the operating theatre, and our baby went straight from the weighing scales and into my arms.

While Shaaron recovered from the operation over the next few days, I slept on a stretcher bed on the floor of her hospital room, our baby tucked beside me, which often caused shrieks of shock from nurses who stumbled in for the 2 a.m. change of shift. It was a great system – Shaaron knew our baby was close and safe, not off in a nursery somewhere, and I could hand her up to Mum for a feed at any time. Sometimes a nurse would discreetly ask Shaaron if this was what she really wanted. She would smile and say, 'Yes, of course!'

Fighting to Be a Dad

The experience of my daughter's birth showed in a way what it is like to be a dad these days – you have to make a firm stand, sometimes even fight, to be allowed to be a dad. The world doesn't seem to want

you to be an involved parent: it would rather have you stay late at the office. Someone else will teach your children to hit a ball, play the piano and believe in themselves – you just pay the bills.

Luckily, fathers are fighting their way back into family life, and very welcome they are, too. Twentieth-century fathering was something of a disaster. Our fathers' generation included a few great dads, but most men of previous generations proved their love by working, not by playing, cuddling, talking or teaching – the things that kids really love. In those hard times of poverty and war, some dads were violent, scary or drank too much. Many were traumatised and were hard to get close to. Some men simply walked out on their families and never came back. So when we come to fathering our own children, it can feel strange, since we may have little knowledge of what good fathering looks like. We only have half the pieces of the jigsaw.

But things are looking up. We know from studies across the developed world that fathers have increased the time they spend with children by 400 per cent since the 1970s.[1] Young dads today are determined to spend more time with their kids, and most of them succeed. In fact, with fatherhood, you never 'fail', as long as you don't quit. As long as you are willing to have a go, you will always achieve more than you realise. Don't be tempted to leave all the parenting to your partner. As we'll see in this chapter, men bring different things to parenting to what women bring, things that are unique and irreplaceable. The more you do with your kids, the more you will rediscover your talents at fathering and your own unique style. There is nothing as satisfying as raising great kids.

Reviving a Lost Art

A lot of fathering of boys is simple. Here are some clues:

- Most boys love to be physically active, to have fun with their fathers. They love to hug their dad, and play-wrestle with him. (If they don't like it, you're probably being too rough!)
- They like to accompany you on adventures and experiences in the big, wide world – all the while feeling secure because Dad seems so huge and capable (even if he doesn't feel that way himself half of the time).
- They love to hear stories about your life, meet your friends, and see what you do for a living.
- They love you to teach them things – anything, really. If you don't know about things like fishing, making stuff in sheds or go-karts, then choose something that interests you and might suit their age and stage as well. It's trying that counts.

Kids Learn Your Attitudes

Kids don't just learn from what you say to them, they take on your attitudes as well. A friend of mine, a Vietnam veteran, was driving with his children and pulled up at some traffic lights. An Asian family were among those crossing at the

MIRROR NEURONS

Mirror neurons were first discovered in 1996. These are a network of nerve cells that run alongside our motor nerves, and they have a unique role. They mirror, or imitate, everything we watch. So if we watch ballet, or football, or someone having a passionate kiss, our mirror neurons practise this action. The mirror actions are stored in our brain, ready to make it easier to copy what we've seen. (So every couch potato really does have an inner athlete, or rock star, or red-hot lover eagerly trying to get out!) This, we now know, is the reason that we can learn skills as fast as we do. But it's a two-edged sword, because it means that everything kids see, they take into their brains and are inclined to repeat. The ramifications of this are huge.

This certainly impacts on what we might allow children to watch on television and in computer games, and it underlines the importance of not depicting violence or violent sex in the media. But it especially impacts on how we behave around our kids. If children see us always being grumpy, self-pitying, sneaky, lying and cheating, vicious or mean, they become that. They take in our actions, but also our moods and outlook. Many a man has been horrified to notice he has the same gestures, movements or expressions that his father used to have. Or he comes out with words or sayings that his old man used to use. Psychologists hear this all the time in their consulting room: 'I hate the guy, and now I am turning out just like him.' This is not genetic, it's 'mirror learning'. It's a good reason to really work on how you act around your kids.

lights. My friend's four-year-old, strapped into his booster seat in the back, suddenly made a racist comment! My friend recognised his own words, and was shocked to hear them from a child: they sounded ugly and wrong to him. He found a parking spot and pulled over. He told his child he was sorry he had ever spoken like that, and he didn't want the child ever to speak like that either.

Kids Learn to Love by Watching You

Children even learn about love by watching you. They love it when you show warmth to their mother, give her a compliment, flirt, exchange a cuddle or a kiss. Most small children cannot resist squeezing in whenever they see their parents hugging. They love to

soak in the feeling of the two of you. When you are private, and close the bedroom door, children even learn from this some of the awe and mystery of love.

Being respectful to their mother is important. So is being self-respecting – not getting into abusive or nasty arguments. Your son needs to see not only that women are never abused, but that a man can argue calmly, without fighting or lashing out.

Kids Learn to Feel by Watching You

Sons learn how to express their feelings by watching their fathers and other men. They need to see you showing all four of the basic feelings:

1. Sadness – when someone has died or a disappointment has come along
2. Anger – when something has been unjust or wrong
3. Happiness – when things go well, and
4. Fear – when there is danger.

Dads have to show real care in expressing feelings around their children. The reason for this is that dads and mums are the pillars of a child's world. Children don't want to see those pillars come tumbling down. So while they need to know and see when we are angry, scared, happy or sad, they also want to know that we can 'hold' those feelings. This means that we can be afraid, but not rattled; mad, but not dangerous; happy, but not stupid; and sad, but not overwhelmed or dismayed. They don't really want to see us losing our grip. But they are touched and helped if we can shed a tear or honestly express anger or fear, because they have those emotions all the time.

Often, when men have an uncomfortable feeling, they will convert it into something more comfortable. Usually anger is the most comfortable feeling for men. When your little boy has got lost in the shopping centre or your teenager has taken a foolish risk, a father who can say, 'I was scared', has much more impact than one who yells and slams doors. If men act angry when they are really sad, scared or even happy, this can be pretty confusing for kids.

Boys are trying to match their inner sensations with outer ways of behaving, and they need us to show them how this is done.

Whatever Happens in Your Marriage, Don't Divorce Your Kids

Divorce is a huge blow to a father's hopes and dreams for his children. Some men feel so grief-stricken that they cut and run. Others have to fight the system to stay in contact with their children. It's vitally important – whatever happens to your marriage – that you stay in your children's lives. More and more fathers are sharing parenting equally (or more) after divorce. I've talked to men who, after divorce, decided it would be simpler for the children if they didn't maintain contact. They always profoundly regretted this decision.

There are some great organisations for separated dads that have sprung up, which are mostly constructive and very helpful. Also divorce courts are now more aware that kids need fathers in their lives, and will work to make sure that contact is shared and maintained.

~ WHO WAS THAT MASKED MAN?

For your children's sake, if your marriage comes to an end, learn to be polite and kind to your ex-partner, even if you don't always feel it. Better still, work to preserve your partnership by giving that some time and attention too, before it's too late.

Rough-and-tumble Games: What's Really Going On?

There's a unique father behaviour that has been observed all over the world. Dads (along with big brothers, uncles and grandpas) love to wrestle and play rough-and-tumble games with little boys. They can hardly resist it. The men and the big boys get the little boys and throw them about. The little boys come running back and say, 'Do it again!' Sydney counsellor Paul Whyte puts it very plainly: 'If you want to get along with boys, learn to wrestle!'[2]

For a long time nobody understood why this was so – especially mothers, who are usually trying to calm things down, while dads seem likely to stir them up all over again! But it's been found that what boys are learning in 'rough and tumble' is an essential lesson for all males: how to be able to have fun, get noisy, even get angry and, at the same time, know when to stop. For a male, living with testosterone, this is vital. If you live in a male body, you have to learn how to drive it.

The Big Male Lesson: Knowing When to Stop

If you've ever wrestled with a little boy, say a three- or four-year-old, it always starts out happily enough. But often, after a minute or two, he 'loses it'. He gets angry. His little jaw starts to jut out! He knits his eyebrows together and (if you haven't spotted the warning signs yet) starts to get serious and hit out with knees and elbows. Ouch!

A dad who knows what he's doing stops the action right there. 'Hooooold it! Stop!' Then a little lecture takes place – not yelling, just calmly explaining. 'Your body is precious [pointing at boy], and my body is precious too. We can't play this game if somebody might get hurt. So we need a few rules – like, no elbowing and no kneeing or punching! Do you understand? Can you handle it?' (Here's a tip: always say 'Can you handle it?' rather than 'Will you keep to the rules?', which sounds kind of wimpish. No boy is going to say 'no' to a question like 'Can you handle it?')

Then you re-commence. The boy is learning a most important life skill – self-control. He's learning that he can be strong and excited, but can also choose where and when to back off. For males, this is very important. In adult life, a man will usually be stronger than his wife or partner. He must know how to not 'lose it', especially when he is angry, tired and frustrated.

For a marriage to survive, it is sometimes necessary for partners to stand nose to nose, while saying some really honest stuff. This is called 'truth time' – the time when disputes that have been building up get aired and cleared up. (We wrote a book about this called *The Making of Love*.[3])

A woman can't have this kind of honest and intense discussion with a man unless she feels absolutely safe with him. She needs to

know she will never be hit, and he needs to know in himself that he won't hit. (In some marriages, it's the woman who is the violent one, the woman who needs to make this commitment.)

A real man is one who is in charge of himself and his behaviour. A real man can be furiously angry, and yet you can feel utterly safe standing right next to him. That's a tough call. But it begins in this small way, play-wrestling on the back lawn.

Dads can do this, uncles, friends, even mums (though mums don't enjoy it quite as much).

 STORIES FROM THE HEART

WHAT FATHERS DO

(by Jack Kammer[4])

This could be dangerous, I thought. This is Los Angeles. And, besides, it's getting dark.

Stranded and alone, hauling a heavy suitcase along Washington Boulevard east of Lincoln Avenue, unable to find a phone that made sense or a taxi dispatcher interested in my fare, I was running late for my plane at LAX. I decided that this was a chance I needed, no, *wanted* to take. I approached three young Hispanic men standing outside their car in a fast-food parking lot.

But first a little background. I had just spent four days in the mountains above Palm Springs at a conference of men who wanted to give the nation new hope for old and growing problems. We were a few of the big fish in the small pond that some have called 'the Men's Movement'. We agreed that what the nation most urgently needs right now is a massive infusion of strong, noble, loving, nurturing, healthy masculine energy to counteract America's malaise, impotence and social pathologies. We talked a lot about the importance of fathers, both as an archetypal metaphor and as a practical reality.

Back in the fast-food parking lot, I warily approached the three young, black-haired, brown-skinned men.

'How ya doing?' I said calmly and evenly. 'I'm trying to get to LAX and I'm running late. The cabs and the phones aren't cooperating. How much money would you need to take me?'

They looked at each other. One of them in a white T-shirt said to the one who must have been the driver, 'Go for it, man.' The driver hesitated.

I said, 'Name a price that makes it worth your while.'

He looked straight at me. 'Twenty bucks,' he said.

'I'll give you fifty.'

'Let's do it, man,' said the T-shirted youth. The driver nodded and popped the trunk.

'You wanna put your suitcase here?'

'No, thanks,' I answered straight back. The image of being forced empty-handed out of the car was clear in my mind. 'I'd rather keep it with me.'

'That's cool,' 'the T-shirt' said.

So there I was, entrusting my life to what I hoped to be 'positive male energy'. I was thinking we should go west to Lincoln Avenue. We headed east. Now what?

But then we turned south and soon we were on a freeway. I knew it could have been stupid, but I took out my wallet, removed a twenty and said to the driver, 'Here, I want to pay you now.' The driver took it with a simple 'Thanks'.

'So here I am, guys,' I said. 'I sure hope you're going to take care of me.'

T-shirt, sitting in the back seat with me, my suitcase between us, smiled knowingly and said, 'It's OK, man. We're good guys.'

I nodded and shrugged. 'I sure hope so, because if you're not, I'm in big trouble, aren't I?'

They all laughed, and then T-shirt spoke up. 'So where you from?'

'Baltimore,' I answered.

'Oh, man, it's nice back east. That's what they say. Green and everything.'

I smiled and nodded, 'Yeah. And back east, LA is our idea of heaven.'

'Naah, it's rough here, man. It's hard.' T-shirt was clearly going to be the spokesman.

Every issue we men's movement guys had talked about during our conference in the mountains was in this car. It was time for a reality check.

'How old are you guys?' I asked.

They were sixteen and seventeen. They were all in school and had part-time jobs. T-shirt and the driver worked in a restaurant. The quiet young man riding shotgun didn't say.

'Tell me about the gangs. Are there gangs at your school?'

'There's gangs everywhere, man. Everywhere. It's crazy.'

'Are you guys in a gang?' I asked.

'No way, man.'

'Why not?' I wondered.

'Because there's no hope in it. You just get a bullet in your head.'

'Yeah, but what hope is there for you outside the gang?'

'I don't know. I just want to get a future. Do something.'

'What's the difference between you guys and the guys in the gangs?'

'I don't know, man. We just don't want to do it.'

'Yeah, but why not? What's the difference?' I gently pressed.

'I don't know, man. I don't know. We're just lucky I guess.'

I let the question sit for a moment, then started up. 'What about fathers? Do you have a father at home?' I asked the youth in the back seat with me.

'Yeah. I do.'

'How about you?' I asked the driver.

'Yeah, I got a dad.'

'Living with you?'

'Yeah.' And the shotgun rider volunteered, 'I got a dad, too.'

'How about the guys in the gangs? Do they have fathers living with them?'

'No way, man. None of them do.'

'So maybe fathers make a difference?' I suggested.

'Absolutely, man. Absolutely.'

'Why?' I probed. 'What difference does a father make?'

'He's always behind you, man, pushing you. Keeping you in line.' 'Yeah. Telling you what's what,' driver and shotgun agreed.

And I was taken safely right where I needed to go. On time. Without a hitch. The driver even asked what terminal I wanted.

I met eighteen amazing men at the conference in the mountains. I am eternally grateful for their wisdom and their urge to heal the nation. But the most amazing men I met on my trip were these three, Pablo, Juan and Richard – amazing because, in spite of everything, they were trying to be good.

And the men to whom I am most grateful are the men I never met. The men to whom I am most grateful are their fathers. It was their fathers who got me to the airport. It was their fathers who kept me safe.

Teaching Boys to Respect Women

One day, in his early to mid-teens, each boy makes a very important discovery. A light globe goes on above his head. It suddenly occurs to him that he is bigger than his mother! Even the sweetest, gentlest boy just can't help realising, sooner or later: 'She can't make me do it!' The thought leads to action and, sooner or later, a boy will try to get the best of Mum by bluffing or intimidating her, even in subtle ways. This is an important teaching moment. Don't panic, it isn't necessary to worry or get scared.

Picture this if you will. Fourteen-year-old Sam is in the kitchen. Sam's job is to do the dishes – clear them up, scrape them off, put them in the dishwasher and switch it on. No big deal – he's done it since he was eight. But last night, he didn't finish the job. So, tonight, when his mother goes to get the dishes from the dishwasher (to serve up the meal his father has cooked!) they are in there, unwashed, with green fur growing on them.

Sam's mum naturally pulls him up. 'What's happened?' But tonight Sam is fourteen! He heaves his shoulders back, he stalks about. Perhaps he speaks a little disrespectfully to his mother, under his breath.

Now let's imagine this family is really lucky. One, it includes a father. Two, he's home. And, three – he knows his job!

Sam's father is in the lounge room reading the paper (kind of keeping an overview of things). He picks up on what is going on in the kitchen. This is his cue! Something deep inside him has been waiting for this moment! He folds his paper, strides to the kitchen, and leans on the fridge. Sam can *feel* him come in – it's a kind of primeval moment. The father looks long and hard at Sam and says some time-honoured words – words that you probably heard when you were fourteen.

'Don't speak to your mother in that tone of voice ...'

Now, Sam's mother is a twenty-first-century woman, and is quite capable of dealing with Sam. The difference is she is not in it alone. Sam realises that there are two adults here who respect and support each other and who are going to bring him up well. The key feeling is 'gentle but firm'. It's as if they are saying to Sam, 'You are a good kid, but you are not raised yet. We will work together to help you become a fine young man. And we will never give up on you.'

It doesn't even have to be a dad. It could be two women raising this boy. The key thing is that each parent supports the other. You don't have to agree – parenthood is an ongoing conversation. Different points of view are a plus, if you are able to keep talking it through. But never undermine each other.

Most importantly, Sam's mother knows that she does not need to ever feel intimidated in her own home. It's not a physical thing but a kind of moral force. If the father is for real, if he respects his partner and has credibility, then it will work every time, even if some more discussion is needed. The discussion should not be about the dishes, but about how to converse respectfully and safely. (If a mother is raising a boy on her own, things have to take a slightly different tack – this is discussed in the chapter on mothering, 'Mothers and Sons'.)

FATHER TAKING AN OVERVIEW OF THE SITUATION

Sadly, many dads don't get this aspect of their role. I've seen dads come in to this conversation and say, 'why are you picking on the kid?' or 'why are you making such an issue of it, darling?' or 'hey you guys, I can't hear the television!' These dads are undermining their wives. This is a disaster, when a mother is doing the hard stuff, and the father cuts her legs out from under her. These men are in for a terrible time. The gods, and the women, smile on those men who stand alongside them without getting too heavy, and just add their support to the situation.

You Don't Have to Have All the Answers

When I was a young man, I studied martial arts. I was pretty bad at it, but I liked the idea of being able to defend myself and others. Perhaps I would get a chance to rescue a beautiful maiden. The one time I got mugged though, the mugger didn't use any of the attacks I had learnt to defend. I remember thinking, 'Damn, I wish he would attack me the way I was taught!' (Luckily the mugger had terrible timing, and some police actually came round the corner and arrested him in the act.)

Being a father is rather like this. We men think we have to be completely prepared; or worse, we think that if we don't know what to do, there's something wrong with us. But parenthood is all about messing things up. That's how you learn. Kids keep changing, each kid is different, and it's only by messing things up that you get it right. The trick is to keep wide awake and see what works, and change if it doesn't.

As our kids reach new ages and create new challenges, we inevitably lose the plot at times. Can they stay at their new friend's place overnight? Is that film suitable for them to watch? What is a fair consequence for this misbehaviour? Sometimes it's a close call.

What to do? If you don't have an answer on the spot, then it's OK to stall. The best thing to do is simply talk it over with your partner or a friend. If you are both stuck, talk it over with other parents. My kids know that if they hassle me, I am more likely to give an unfavourable decision, so they have become more careful! But if I genuinely don't know what to do or say, I reply, 'Well, I'm not happy about it, but I'll sleep on it and we'll talk some more tomorrow.' As long as you always follow up, this response works well. Family life is a work in progress. You only get in trouble if you 'have to be right' and you 'have to show them who's boss'. If you are human, it goes much better.

Finding the Balance Is Hard

It's OK to be unpopular with your kids once or twice a day! If you have lots of good time together and a long history of care and involvement to draw on, then you have goodwill saved up, like money in the bank. Sometimes dads are around so little, they want it all to be smooth sailing when they *are* there. But kids need to know when they do something wrong. It can be hard to find that middle point between hard and soft. Maybe it's about being clear, and not about using power or force at all.

I have a friend, Paul, who is very close to his kids – I admire and envy how natural a father he is. But he too gets it wrong sometimes. Paul told me once how he 'lost it' with his twelve-year-old son after a nightmare day at work. He exploded over some small thing and sent the boy off to his bedroom, yelling at him as he went. The son deserved hardly any of this, the yelling was louder than was necessary, the boy was wincing in fear – it was a disaster.

Paul stood for minutes, ashamed and red-faced at what he had done. He realised it had to be fixed. He went and sat on the boy's bed. He apologised. The boy said nothing, just lay face down on the bed. But ten minutes later, the father was in the bathroom. The boy walked past him on the way to brush his teeth and get ready for bed. As he passed, he uttered some words that touched his father's heart in a most unforgettable way: 'Why is it so hard to hate you?'

Dads Do Matter

Even today, after a whole revolution in fathers' roles, people still ask: do dads matter? Can't mothers do it all?

The research supporting the importance of dads is overwhelmingly clear.[5] Boys with absent fathers, or with problem fathers, are statistically more likely to be violent, get hurt, get into trouble, do poorly in school, and be members of teenage gangs in adolescence. They are less likely to progress to university or have a good career. They marry less successfully, and are less effective fathers themselves. A good mum can make up for not having a father around, but it's really, really hard work.

Fatherless daughters are more likely to have low self-esteem, to have sex before they really want to, to get pregnant young, be assaulted or abused, and not continue their schooling. Families without men are usually poorer, and children of these families are likely to move downwards on the socio-economic ladder. Is that enough to convince you?

Fathering is the best thing you are ever likely to do – for your own satisfaction and joy, and for its effect on the future of other human beings. And it's good fun.

STORIES FROM THE HEART

IS IT ADHD OR DDD (DAD DEFICIT DISORDER)?

Several years ago, a man called Don came up to me after a lecture, and told me this story. Don was a truck driver and, a year earlier, his son, aged eight, had been diagnosed with Attention Deficit Disorder. Don read the diagnosis and, for want of better information, decided it meant his son Troy wasn't getting enough attention. That, surely, was what 'attention deficit' meant!

Don set himself the goal of getting more involved with Troy. He had always taken the view that raising children was best left to 'the missus' while he worked to pay the bills. Now all of that changed. In the holidays, and after school when possible, Troy rode in the truck with his dad. On weekends, whereas Don had often spent the time away with mates who collected and rode classic motorcycles, Troy now came along too.

'We had to tone down the language and clean up our act a bit, but the blokes all understood, and some started bringing their kids, too,' Don told me with a smile.

The good news: Troy calmed down so much in a couple of months that he came off his Ritalin medication – he wasn't 'ADD' any longer. But father and son continue to hang out together – because they enjoy it.

Note: We are not saying here that all instances of Attention Deficit Disorder are really Dad-deficit disorders – but some are.[6] (For more about ADHD and boys, see Chapter 10.)

STORIES FROM THE HEART

LETTER FROM A FATHER

Dear Steve,

We have had many challenges with our son, and he with us! I'm pleased to say that things are going well for him. Other parents of boys might like to share some things we have learnt.

The biggest difference between Matt and his sister Sophie was that Matt was very impulsive and had explosive energy. When he was eight, he ran straight out in front of a car without even pausing to look. Luckily the driver had seen Matt's ball roll onto the road and was already braking hard! The car just missed him. Boys don't seem to always think before they act.

We really got it wrong with Matt in his early teens. Because his sister had been so easy to negotiate with, we assumed he would be the same. But he just didn't do his housework, his homework, or keep to agreements about when he would be in. Reasoning wasn't enough with him – until we realised he was crying out for firm boundaries and enforced consequences. We had been threatening him, sure, but just not carrying out consequences. When we finally did this consistently (feeling pretty mean sometimes), then he improved out of sight. The thing was, he was happier, too. I think some boys just need this.

Something that really helped Matt was the peer support scheme. In Year 6 at primary school he had a kindergarten child to take care of and protect. This gave him a sense of being important and he came home full of stories about his younger charge – how the little boy learnt, what he got up to. We saw a whole different side to him. Then in Year 7 at high school, he had a Year 11 peer support boy who watched out for him in a bullying situation, so he benefited both ways.

Around this time we learnt that although he was ratty at home, the teachers thought he was great at school! So it was just that he was letting off steam with us. Lots of parents I've talked to recognise this 'school angel–home devil' situation!

At around fourteen and fifteen we felt Matt was drifting into his own world – rarely talking to us, just eating and disappearing, and giving us no insight into his world of school, his friends and so on. Our only communication seemed to be in telling him off. Luckily we always eat dinner together at the table, and this was the one time we got to talk. We resolved to have more time together – father and son weekends away. My wife decided to get out of the negative cycle and to give compliments to Matt, not just criticisms. He responded quite warmly. I think we had just got caught in a negative pattern. Boys do want to be friends; they don't want to live in their own world, which is often quite lonely.

We both benefited from a P.E.T. [Parent Effectiveness Training] course. The best things we learnt were: use 'I messages' (like 'I was scared when you didn't come home at the agreed time. I need you to make agreements you can keep.') instead of 'You are unreliable and useless! You had better come home or else!'; also, how to listen to kids' problems, so they can talk them over, instead of jumping in with advice.

We are a lot happier now, and Matt is a sociable and pleasant young man, instead of a surly boy. It's important never to give up with your kids. Keep learning and getting help if you are stuck. You can always improve things if you try. Kids really need you to keep communicating with them.

Geoff H.

DADS AND DAUGHTERS

It's not the topic of this book, but in case this is the only parenting book you ever read, here is something about girls. Mothers are the security blanket for daughters, their major support system, but dads are the self-esteem department. This is because for most girls, the opposite sex is important, and you are their practice person for the opposite sex.

For this reason, you sometimes have five times the power your spouse has to either bless or wound your daughter. Think of it like a sword: you can either cut, or place it gently on her shoulder and say, 'Arise, Princess'!

So don't ever, whatever you do, criticise her looks, her weight, or any aspect of her appearance. Not ever. You can debate what clothes she might wear if they are too revealing, but even here get her mother's help.

What you can do is spend time with her at sports, activities, even just driving her places, and above all, talk and be interested. Go to a movie with her, stop for a coffee and a chat when you shop together. A dad who is close to his daughter is so good for her, because he becomes the yardstick by which she measures boys. It's as if she knows she is interesting, intelligent and worthwhile. Boys have to measure up to this – which eliminates 80 per cent of them right off! This has to be a good investment!

STORIES FROM THE HEART

FATHER WOUNDS AND MOTHER WOUNDS

I'm staying at a little beachside town called Penguin, in Tasmania, doing talks along the coast in small schools each night. I've just checked into my hotel and gone off to find some lunch. A mum and a small boy of about four are coming out of the shop when suddenly a rain shower starts to pelt down heavy drops. The mum stoops down almost on a level with the boy, smiles at him and says, 'We're gonna have to run! Are you ready?' He grins back, and hand in hand they sprint laughing to their car.

The sense of closeness between the two of them, the fact she is willing to make a pleasure out of something that could have been annoyance, warms my heart. That she has not forgotten what fun life can be just tells you – this little boy is having a great childhood. I hope that one day every little kid can have a mum and dad who delight in their existence.

Most kids have loving parents, and though we all make mistakes or have bad-tempered times, within reason that just lets our kids know we are human too. But some have dads or mums who are caught in terrible patterns of negativity, and do real harm. Some kids have father-wounds, some have mother wounds, some have both. We shouldn't shy away from calling this what it is, and getting help if we recognise this might be us.

As a small boy, I lived in fear of the class bully, Joe Woulfe. Joe was in my Grade 1 class, in a part of northern England which sat between the wild moorlands and the grim industrial area of Teesside. Joe Woulfe would hit you as soon as look at you. Then one day something happened. My dad and I were out on the grassy reserve by the sea where fairground rides would visit in the summer, when I saw Joe with his dad. Red-faced, head thrust forward, jaw jutting, sleeves rolled up, this dad stalked ahead of his son, who suddenly looked small and afraid. Even at my age I saw that this boy's home life would have been frightening, that I would not want to be him, that there were reasons behind his continual aggression. He was poor, frightened, and unsafe and I felt for him.

In the twentieth century, fathering was very fraught. The effects of wars, economic depressions and the industrialisation of life and work took men out of family life and crushed or brutalised them. Millions had post-traumatic stress from their war experiences, and a shut-down dad prone to drunken or furious rage was a feature of family life in every street. When I was a child, you could hear family violence ringing out on a still night in the way you can now hear music or television.

It was the father–son relationship that was most damaged by this, for boys need to feel cared about by their dads. In my book *Manhood*[7] I wrote that only one in ten men in the twentieth century was actually close to his dad. Many were completely estranged, or at best dutiful but wooden. By the time they reached their mid-teens most young men could not wait to escape their dads. And that's if the dads had not already abandoned them. I had a warm and caring dad, who was an exception to his environment. But I saw so much damage around me that the revival, or creation, of warm affectionate fatherhood became my life's work.

Today's dad who plays happily and safely with his kids, who doesn't hit or hurt them or call them names, is a wonderful change. A man who can sort out differences respectfully and in a relaxed way with his partner, hang in through sexual ups and downs, and understand and sympathise with a woman's emotional world as well as express and be in touch with his own; who talks to his friends instead of the bottom of a beer glass and gains courage and spirit to be his own self; who finds happy work, and doesn't become trapped in the corporate machine – this kind of dad is on the rise. Please read *Manhood* if you are a man who wants to be like this, or a woman who wants her husband to be one.

The father wound that ran like a Grand Canyon through the twentieth century did incalculable harm. Men reading this will know what it was like. And in fact remembering our own boyhoods and what they lacked is the answer – if we can feel the pain of our own childhood, then that's the starting point in making it different for our own sons and daughters. We won't want them to feel like we did. And we will start looking for how to do it differently.

THE MOTHER WOUND

Maggie Dent, a wonderful advocate of boys, says that a small number have very challenged and difficult relationship with mothers. As a result, they are likely to spin off the rails in one of two ways – to become violent and untrusting, woman-addicted but woman-hating at the same time. Or they may be self-destructive, suicidal and despairing. A mum who doesn't love you is not a good start in life, and yet some mothers, for reasons really beyond their control, can struggle with maternal attachment and bondedness.[8]

If you feel this applies, even a little, to you, then getting counselling help of a concerted kind is absolutely key. We all at some stage in life need to get some love and care coming to us if we are to give it out to our children.

Maggie believes that the culture has to step up around boys who are not in happy relationships with mums. That we need solid, older women – school teachers often fill this role, or grandmothers or professionals in youth work or the like, who step in and give warm strong containment to boys spinning out of control. We have put too much weight onto our fragile little nuclear families, and a circle of outer supports have to be brought into action to hold boy energies and needs. If we don't provide warm father and mother figures then the drug dealer or the gang leader will substitute, and we all know how that ends.

IN A NUTSHELL

- Make the time to be a dad. In society today, men are often little more than walking wallets. You have to fight to be a real father to your kids.
- Be active with your children – talk, play, make things, go on trips together. Take every chance you can to interact.
- Sometimes A(Attention) Deficit Disorder is actually D(Dad) Deficit Disorder.
- Share the discipline with your partner. Often your son will respond more readily to you – not from fear, but from respect and wanting to please you. Don't hit or frighten boys – it just makes them mean to others.
- A boy will copy you. He will copy your way of acting towards his mother. He will take on your attitudes (whether you are a racist, a perpetual victim, an optimist or a person who cares about justice, and so on). And he will only be able to show his emotions if you can show yours.
- Most boys love rough-and-tumble games. Use these for enjoyment and also to teach him self-control, by stopping and setting some rules whenever the game gets too rough.
- Teach your son to respect women – and to respect himself.

Chapter 6

Mothers and Sons

This chapter was co-written with Shaaron Biddulph

Remember that first, quiet moment, when your new baby boy was lying in your arms and you got your first real chance to look at him – gazing at his little face and body?

For mothers, it sometimes takes a while to realise that you really have a son, a boy. Most women say they feel more confident with a baby girl. They feel they would intuitively know what her needs will be. But a boy! At the birth of a son, some women will exclaim in horror, 'I don't know what to *do* with a boy!' However well prepared we are rationally, the emotional response is often still, 'Wow! This is unknown territory!'

The Mother's Background

Right from the start, a woman's own 'male history' has an effect on her mothering. We needlessly, unconsciously set huge store on what sex a baby is. Many people can't even really relate to a baby until they ask what kind it is. This shouldn't matter, but it does.

Every time a mother looks at her baby boy, hears him crying for her or changes his nappy, she is aware that he's male. So, whatever maleness has meant to her will now come into the foreground.

A woman remembers her dad and how he treated her. She has the experience of brothers, cousins and the boys she knew at school. And then all the men she has known – lovers, teachers, bosses, doctors, ministers, co-workers and friends. All these are woven into

her 'male history', colouring her attitude to this unsuspecting little baby boy!

Her ideas on 'what men are like', 'how men have treated me' and 'what I would want to be different about men' all begin to affect how she acts towards her child.

As if that wasn't enough, her feelings about this baby's father also complicate the picture. As he grows up, does he look like his father? Does that make her love him more? If she is no longer with his father, or if there are problems, this can colour her feelings, too. A woman may be very aware of all these feelings, or this entire process might be totally unconscious.

How We Care for Our Baby Boys

All our earlier attitudes and beliefs about males will be reflected in our everyday care for our boys – each time we rush to help, or we hold back in order to let them do it for themselves; each time we encourage or discourage them; each time we cuddle them warmly or frown at them and walk away. All our responses arise from our internal attitudes towards having a baby – and having a *male* baby.

It's a big help if you adopt a curious attitude – of wanting to learn and understand about a boy's world. As a woman, you cannot know what it's like to be in a male body. If you didn't have brothers (or a dad who was involved), then you have to get more information to find out what is normal in boys. It's good to be able to ask your partner or male friends for information. Sometimes you just need practical knowledge.

Mums Help with Learning About the Opposite Sex

A mother teaches a boy a great deal about life and love. She is invaluable for helping him gain confidence with the opposite sex. She is his 'first love', and needs to be tender, respectful and playful, without wanting to own or dominate his world. As he gets to school age, she encourages him, helps him make friends, and gives him clues about how to get on well with girls.

Many boys and girls have trouble getting along with the opposite sex, as do many men and women. A mother can make sure her son is not like this; she can help him to relax around girls and women. She can teach him what girls like – they love a boy who can converse, who has a sense of humour, who is considerate, who has his own ideas and opinions, but is interested in theirs, and so on. She can even alert him to the fact that girls can sometimes be mean or thoughtless – that girls are no saints, either.

STORIES FROM THE HEART

LETTER FROM A MOTHER

Dear Steve,

Reading _Raising Boys_, I wanted to add some things I feel so strongly about.

To all the mothers out there – boys are different. So persevere in getting to understand and know them. Don't, whatever you do, give up. Or become resigned and join the anti-boy group, with their weak jokes and tales of woe and 'What can I do?' sort of attitudes. There is a meeting point between mothers and sons. It's up to you. It may not be obvious, it may take time and a number of attempts. Struggle is not a sign of failure, but of something new being born. Look for the good in your son. You will find it.

Boys have tender feelings, and mothers have an essential part in keeping the child whole. Seeing how affectionate they can be at times makes you love them so much more. Give them a chance to play with and help younger children, and to look after animals. See how loving they can be.

Share your son's passions. Tom (my nine-year-old) and I have a wintertime ritual. On a Saturday afternoon we go to the second half of the local football game (which is about the right amount of time for us) and get in for free. We generally sit down by the fence near the try line, close enough to feel the earth and air move as the players surge past. Tom takes great pleasure in telling me who the players are and the rules, and I notice he often tells me the details he knows will interest me, like something about their lives outside football! The action is great, so vigorous and determined. The atmosphere at the historic ground is friendly and excited, a bubble of warmth on a cold afternoon. So different to watching it on the telly! It's an urban adventure.

Boys often need help in connecting with things – a piece of work at school, with using the library, computers, newspapers, encyclopaedias.

Help them to organise their homework, partition the task into 'do-able' chunks, set realistic goals and help them to get there. Make the task smaller so they can relate to it, so they don't feel overwhelmed and give up. At the same time, don't take over – make sure they have the joy of their own achievement.

Expand your boys' awareness, By walking, talking, noticing things, collecting things; by seeing how a tree changes with the seasons, or how a building project is developing. Show them how food happens – planning the purchases, choosing the fruit, the preparation and enjoyment of new foods. Involve them in planning family events and holidays. Show them how to combine their interests with those of others when planning.

Make sure they get enough sleep and a balance of social and quiet time. This is basic but critical. Embrace bedtime rituals, stories, cuddles, tickling on the back, whatever, so they feel safe, loved and at peace. A shared repertoire of favourite stories is invaluable.

Finally, you can really help your sons by supporting their relationship with their father. Fathers may not foresee and plan in the way you do, and this may limit their opportunities to what is nearest at hand. Gentle reminders can be appreciated. Put good men in the path of your son – a groovy music teacher, a valued handyman, a friend's brother. Speak to them about good men, their qualities, and what you notice about how they act in different situations.

Recall their past – tell them what beautiful babies they were, what their births meant to you, what rays of sunshine they are in your life.

A deep harmony … a beautiful boy.

With warm wishes
JT

As mentioned, the opposite-sex parent often holds the key to self-esteem for a growing child. Teenage daughters need to have their image of themselves as intelligent and interesting people boosted by their father. He can also teach them to change a wheel, fix a computer or catch fish. A son whose mother enjoys him as a companion learns that he can be friends with girls comfortably in the years from five to fifteen. The pressure to pair up and prove oneself sexually is taken away, and he can move more naturally through friendship to a deeper connection with a girl when he is ready.

Promoting a Good Self-image

Many boys become painfully awkward by the time they are in high school. They seem ashamed of being male, big and full of hormones. (The media often portrays males as rapists, murderers, or inadequate fools, so a boy may easily feel quite bad about himself as a masculine being.)

Mothers can do a lot to overcome this. I've heard beautiful comments from mothers to their sons: telling them from the age of about ten and upwards, 'wow, you are a great-looking guy!' when they try on their new clothes; or, 'the girl who marries you is going to be so lucky' when they do a good job around the house; and 'I really enjoy your company', 'you're interesting to talk to', and 'you have a really great sense of humour'. From these comments, the boy learns what girls like, and becomes more able to approach them in a relaxed and equal way.

PRACTICAL HELP

LITTLE BOYS' BODIES

Penises and testicles are a bit of a mystery to mothers. Here are a doctor's answers to some questions mothers commonly ask:

Q: Should my son have two testicles visible?
A: *By the time of the 'six-week check' that all babies should get from the health visitor or doctor, both testicles should be able to be seen.*

Q: Is it OK to touch his penis to wash it?
A: *Of course! You have to wash around the penis and testicles when changing nappies and in the bath. Once out of nappies, a little boy can wash his own penis while you supervise.*

Q: Should I pull back the foreskin to keep his penis really clean?
A: *This is not necessary, in fact it's not a good idea at all. At this age the foreskin is adhered to the end of the penis. Toddlers naturally pull back their foreskin little by little, and at about three or four years of age you will notice that it retracts. At the age of four, you can tell him from time to time in the bath to pull it back and wash around the end of the penis. Show him how to leave the foreskin back until he is dry after a shower, and how to pull the foreskin back when having a wee so as to keep urine from staying underneath it.*

Q: My son pulls and stretches his penis or pushes his finger inside it. Is this OK?
A: *Basically children won't damage themselves, because if it hurts they'll soon stop! Penises are a little fascinating to their owners, feel comforting to hold, and this is fine. Don't make a fuss about it.*

Q: My son often holds onto his penis to stop himself weeing. Is that harmful?

A: *Most boys do this. Girls have strong pelvic muscles that can hold back their wee without anyone knowing they're doing it. Boys are made differently, and can't do this. So if they need to do a wee but are too engrossed in playing, they will often 'hang on'. Encourage them to take a toilet break!*

Q: What name should we call our child's penis?

A: *Call a penis a penis. Don't make up silly names for it.*

Q: When boys are a little older, they sometimes get hit in the testicles during games. What should I do?

A: *Testicles are very sensitive – that's why all the men crouch over in sympathy if someone gets hit in the crotch during a cricket match. But usually there is no lasting damage. Go with your boy to a private spot and check him out gently. If there is severe pain, swelling, bleeding, bruising, or if pain continues to make him cry for a long time, or if he vomits, then get him straight to a doctor. Otherwise just let him sit quietly and recover. If tenderness continues after a few hours, have him checked by a doctor.*

If you are in any doubt on these questions, talk to your doctor. It's always best to be on the safe side. Always encourage children to be careful of each other's bodies. Challenge your son or daughter strongly if they think harming other kids is funny or trivial. Come down hard on games that involve grabbing or hitting people in the genitals. Some television shows treat these injuries as a joke, which they are not. Being hit in the genitals is about as funny as being hit in the breasts, and testicles are far more sensitive.

(Our thanks to Dr Nick Cooling of the University of Tasmania for verifying and expanding this advice.)

STORIES FROM THE HEART

AT THE SHOPS

Julie and her son Ben, aged eight, were in town to do some supermarket shopping. Just outside the shop they saw two girls from Ben's class at school, sitting on the bench. Ben gave a cheery 'hi' to the girls, but instead of saying 'hi' back, both girls just looked at the ground and giggled!

Julie and Ben finished their shopping and went on down the street. Julie noticed that Ben was rather quiet, and asked how he was going. 'Oh, I'm fine,' said Ben (who, after all, is an Australian male and obliged to say this!)

Julie wasn't put off. 'Did it upset you that those girls just laughed and didn't say hello?'

'Umm … yes,' admitted Ben.

Julie thought for a moment before replying. 'Hmm, well I don't know if it helps, but I remember being a girl in Third Grade. You did have your favourite boy. But it was kind of awkward. If he spoke to you, especially if you had friends around, you might get embarrassed. So you just might giggle to cover it up. I don't know if that fits here or not.'

Ben didn't say anything, but he seemed to be walking taller all of a sudden!

'Anyhow, it's lucky,' Julie went on, 'that we've forgotten the milk. So we have to go back!' And before Ben could even gasp, she swung round right there on the footpath and headed back to the supermarket. 'You'll get a second chance!' she added. The girls were still there. This time they gave their own cheery 'hi', and Ben had a conversation with them while his mother searched for the milk – which took a while to find!

Adjusting Your Mothering to His Growing Up

As a boy grows from helpless baby to towering teenager, your parenting style has to adjust with him. To begin with, you're 'the boss', providing constant supervision. In the school years you teach, monitor and set limits. Later, you are a consultant and friend as he makes his own way. You gradually allow more and more responsibility and freedom. It's all in the timing. Here are some clues to this.

The Primary School Years

In the primary school years a lot of gentle steering and helping goes on. Mothers watch their sons' activities for dangers or for a lack of balance. They set a limit to television viewing and computer time, so that boys get out and get some exercise. (Many schools have banned computer 'play' in lunch breaks because some boys never learn to socialise or interact – skills they really need.)

Encourage your son to invite friends over, and be kind to and chat with them. Feeding them always helps! Ask them for their points of view and their ideas about school and their lives.

It's OK and important to monitor and check who will be there when your son visits a friend's house. Are they well supervised? Boys can get into deep water if no one looks out for them at this age. They shouldn't be left alone in a house for long under the age of ten (though this depends a lot on where you live). Riding bikes around is not good after dark. And under ten, boys are not yet ready for the traffic on main roads. Their peripheral (sideways) vision is not yet fully developed for judging traffic speeds.

At Secondary School

By secondary school, living with a boy is more a matter of fair exchange – 'I'll drive you there if you help me out here', 'If you cook, I'll clean up'. A boy can accept the clear separation of his activities from yours. But stay friendly and available so that talking can still happen. Be sure to still have special times one-to-one. Stop for a drink and talk on shopping trips. Go out to the movies together, and have time after to talk.

Some boys still love cuddles at this age, while others find it too intrusive. Find ways to show affection that are respectful of his wishes. Sit close on the couch, stroke his head at bedtime, tickle him – find the ways that he doesn't mind.

You may have to make a stand against a school or a sport wanting to dominate your kid's life too much. (See 'Homework Hell', page 163).

Towards the end of high school, around the pressured time of major exams, help your son to study, but take a position that this is not the meaning of life, and that enjoyment and soul-time are also important. Let him know that his worth is not measured by exam results.

In Australia a kind of competitive madness has developed around Year 12 exams. They're portrayed as the make-or-break year of a person's life. We can blaze a middle road here, encouraging kids to give school their best shot (all through late secondary school) but keeping it in proportion with the real goals of adolescence

BASKETBALL IS TOMORROW!

– which are to find what work you really love to do, while also developing socially and creatively.

Here are some points to consider:

- Kids who get high Year 12 scores often bomb out at university, because they aren't motivated by an actual interest in the subjects.[1]
- Courses like medicine are starting to look for more balanced students who have done other degrees first or had other life experiences. Good exam results alone don't make good doctors.
- Well-balanced youngsters are happier, healthier and more likeable employees, and become more successful in professional careers.
- Other courses and careers (such as teaching, nursing and ecology) can offer happier lifestyles and more human satisfaction than highly competitive fields like law, medicine and economics.

Learning Through Consequences

Adolescence is the age of building personal responsibility – which has to be learnt through consequences. For instance, when he starts high school, help your son get organised with books and catching the bus or train. But once he knows how, after a while, it's up to him if he takes the wrong book or misses the transport and is late. He'll soon learn!

Discipline works by cooperation. Natural consequences and a sense of fairness are your tools. Negotiate with him. You can't *make* a teenager do things by force – but you provide so many services that your bargaining power is huge!

Single Mothering: Avoiding Conflicts that Do Harm

For a mother on her own, the mid-teens are an important time to renegotiate what is happening. Boys at this age are wanting to test their strength and gain some independence. For a couple, this is easier – a boy can fight with his dad but know his mother still loves him (and vice versa). But if Mum is the only source of love *and* discipline, it takes real care.

Many mothers have told us, 'I have to keep switching to and fro – being hard and soft, hard and soft. It's really tiring.' (Yet it's still better than having a partner who contradicts you and undermines your discipline.) It's important never to let things get as far as a yelling or hitting match with your son. At this age, while he is learning

to handle his own energies and feelings, he might hurt you and feel terrible afterwards. If you can see a discussion turning into a shouting match or a physical fight, then do the following:

1. Tell him *you* need to calm down. If you can both sit down and talk it over rationally, then do that.
2. If you are feeling too angry or upset, tell him that you will come back to the subject later, when you feel less emotional.
3. Go and sit down or go to another room.
4. Try to act before you are actually 'upset' – if you wait till you are crying or very angry, he will feel guilty and confused.
5. Later in the day, have a talk with him. Set aside the original problem for now. Talk about the issue of being able to get along well in the household and how important that is. Ask if he, too, wants to get along well. Explain that this sometimes involves compromises. The things you *won't* compromise on are those concerning safety, your son keeping agreements he makes, and respecting the rights of others in the family. Ask if he is willing to always stop and calm down if you ask him to do so. Then you can either have a break to celebrate, or talk about the original problem.

By doing something like this, you are saying, in effect, 'for a mother and a teenage son, it's necessary to make some truces, because the situation is delicate'.

If your son is hitting you or intimidating you, get help from a counsellor and/or the police. A single mother is the main source of love for a boy or a girl, and if they hurt or harm you, you will both feel very bad. Yet growing up requires testing limits with someone. Ideally, uncles or adult friends of yours whom the boy trusts may talk to him about treating you with respect. If they can do this without laying a big guilt trip on him, that's great. Hopefully, this is a stage when uncles or grandfathers will be spending time with him, so they may already have his trust and respect.

PRACTICAL HELP

INTRODUCING A NEW PARTNER

Divorce can be tough on a boy, and if his mother finds a new partner, this can also be a big adjustment to make. In his book, *The Wonder of Boys*, Michael Gurian offers some guidelines for mothers who are remarrying after divorce.[2] Please note that these are controversial for many readers, and so just use them as a spark for your own thinking, and not rules to be followed.

1. *Take care with dating behaviour* A mother shouldn't expose her son to myriad male influences. If she dates, she should do so mostly when the son is away at his dad's place. She should only bring a new man into the boy's life when she (and her new man) are really ready to invest in a long-term attachment.
2. *Don't displace Dad* The new partner should not be seen as a substitute for Dad. His role is different. Discipline structures and household routines that are imposed by the stepfather have to be explained clearly to the son and imposed as additions, not substitutes for his father's and mother's rules and routines.
3. *Mend fences with Dad* Strengthened by the new relationship, a mother should confront her part in the marriage break-up, mend fences with the father, and include him in plans and arrangements. Both she and the father should rise above any difficult situations between them for the good of the boy. (Except, of course, in those cases where there is danger or where the birth father wants nothing to do with his child.)
4. *Support living with Dad* The mother may, when the son asks for it, let him go and live with his dad. As the boy moves into his teens, she may need to offer this so that the son will feel OK about asking. Be sensitive that he knows he is still welcome not to go too. And only do this if you are sure that his dad is responsible and safe.

5. *Ensure your new man is not a competitor* A mother needs to reassure her son that he is irreplaceable in her life. She does this with her time, words and actions, not by buying his approval with gifts or treats.

The golden rules are: keep communicating, keep your family rituals strong, and spend time together as parent and child. The greatest gift that parents can give a son in this situation is their own stability.

PRACTICAL HELP

BOYS IN THE KITCHEN

It's easy to kick-start in your kids a lifetime interest in food preparation, because nature is on your side. Kids love to eat. They love the smells, colour, tastes and even the mess of food!

Babies can sit on the floor in the kitchen rolling oranges around or piling pea pods in and out of a plastic bowl. Toddlers can help you to make play dough (not to eat!), stirring and kneading the mixture, adding bright colouring. Then they can have hours of fun playing with the results.

For four- or five-year-olds, Christmas and party treats are the most motivating cooking (because you get to eat them!). Making chocolate crispy cakes and biscuits and icing a cake are all good kids' activities. Never let them near a stove or hot things on their own, though.

Little boys can stir, pour, measure or weigh, peel sweetcorn, shell peas, and wash carrots and potatoes in a plastic bowl. (Growing vegetables in the garden is another great possibility. Radishes grow the fastest. Mangetout, cherry tomatoes and strawberries are also good because you can pick them very frequently.) Boys love to make faces on bread with strips of carrot and celery, sliced tomato and cheese shapes.

They also love freezing juice to make their own 'icy poles'. When a little older, they can use a peeler safely on veggies to help out at dinnertime.

Kids need to be around ten years old before they can use sharp knives, hot liquids or stoves. You should teach them, watch how they go, then check that they are still being careful. One child only in the kitchen is a good idea with hot things.

MEALS BOYS LIKE TO COOK

- Pizzas – buy or make the bases and let them add a variety of toppings
- grills – grilled fish fingers, chicken, sausages, chops or tofu
- pancakes and omelettes
- tossed salads
- hamburgers or steak sandwiches with salad
- pasta and bottled sauce
- roast lamb or chicken (some instruction for this may be helpful)
- stir-fried vegetables and rice, and
- tuna patties made with mashed potato, canned tuna and grated carrot or celery.

Be sure to show lots of pride in their work *and* your appreciation of their help in the kitchen. Show them how they can make a gift (such as a cake or a batch of fresh biscuits) for someone they like. And don't forget that they also need to see their dad working in the kitchen or at the tuck shop at school.

OTHER SAFETY TIPS
Teach your boys to:

- roll up their sleeves and wear an apron (or clothes that won't brush against a hot plate and catch fire)
- wash their hands before they start!
- handle knives with lots of care
- be alert to what gets hot and stays hot during cooking (and to use an oven mitt for picking up hot things)
- turn saucepan handles to the side of the stove where no one can bump them and where a toddler cannot grab them, and clean up spilt food straight away (so they won't slip in it!).

BOYS AND HOUSEWORK

There are several reasons why housework is very good for boys!

PREPARING THEM FOR INDEPENDENT LIVING

It's not healthy for a boy to go from a mother to a partner in one step. An interval of independent living is strongly advised. During this time, he will sometimes need to iron and vacuum and prepare something to eat! These skills should be learnt during the formative younger years, lest serious learning disabilities like 'kitchen blindness' or 'dyslaundria' begin to develop.

In late teens these skills will play a critical role in other ways, too: housework skills are up there with a sports car in the 'chick-magnet' stakes. As a general rule, only cook and clean and tidy for your son if you want him to stay at home for the rest of your life!

Even marriage cannot be relied upon to solve your son's domestic problems. The woman (or man) he eventually links up with in this post-modern world may not be inclined to be a household servant to your son. There's a distinct and frightening possibility that he will have to do his share on a lifelong basis!

ENCOURAGING REAL SELF-ESTEEM

From the moment you first see a television screen or a billboard, your mental health is under attack.

We all see about 3,000 advertising messages a day,[3] and they all tell us we are not good enough, and should be dissatisfied with our looks and our life. Advertising attacks your children's mental health: it tells them that self-esteem is about how you look and what you own. The sports stars and fashion models our kids admire actually have terrible self-esteem – they know that their fame can disappear overnight. So how do we make our kids feel good about themselves? The secret is easy: teach them to be useful.

It's important to tell kids they are great, smart, and able to think and figure things out. But that's only the first step. Being able to cook a meal, iron a shirt, look after a pet, mow enough lawns to buy a computer, or hold down a part-time job are all sources of indestructible pride. We should give our kids lots of chances to experience their capabilities.

As a guideline, we suggest teaching your son to prepare a complete evening meal every week by the time he is ten. Perhaps start with pasta and bottled sauce, and a simple dessert. (Don't have boys handling boiling water earlier than nine years of age, as they aren't coordinated enough to do it safely. Nine is the age that a boy's attention span overtakes that of a border collie! Under nine, they can prepare things and clean up, but you do the cooking.) Little boys from about five onwards should start setting out the cutlery for meals and finding and folding their clothes from the laundry pile. Seven-year-olds can clear up the table, and so on.

Something remarkable happens in families where boys are given this chance to be useful by cooking. When a teenage boy experiences the pride of being useful to his family, and then later to his relatives and to the wider circle of people who like and respect him, he tastes the special joy of earning respect through making a contribution. Once tasted, he

will never lose that feeling. If a boy gets hold of the joy of being useful, it will affect his values for life and all that goes with that – which friends he chooses, his choice of subjects at school, his girlfriends and eventual wife, and his career. So you can see just how important that first batch of pasta and bottled sauce is going to be![4]

CREATING A CHANCE TO GET CLOSE

There's another reason to teach your boys housework on a regular basis, which may surprise you – conversation.

Boys rarely leap into frank and honest discussions of their educational progress, friendship traumas or love life the minute they walk in the door. This has long been a source of frustration to mothers and fathers keen to catch up with their son's life. Males like to talk 'sideways' rather than face to face. This gives them time to search for the right words, and avoids that embarrassing eyeball-to-eyeball stuff that women like to engage in.

If you want to get close to your son and help him to offload his worries or share his joys, you have to do things together. In modern life, that usually means housework. Whether you are helping your son whip up a delicious soufflé for dinner or teaching him how to get a really good shine on the shower cubicle later that night, these are the times that he will begin to tell you about his problems with maths or the girl who is chasing him.

Doing work with your son – teaching him the tricks of doing it well, how to be fast and efficient and happy in making life cleaner and tidier – is a way that a parent and child can enjoy each other, have good long talks, and pass on all kinds of wisdom. If you do all the housework for your son, then you miss out and so does he.

STORIES FROM THE HEART

MAKING ROOM FOR A DAD TO GROW

Dear Steve,

I'm writing this because I thought you would enjoy hearing about the impact of your book, *Manhood*, on our family. It can all be summed up in one particular scene, which still sits so clearly in my mind.

My husband, Joe, and I were sitting at a table outside a restaurant at our usual holiday location on the South Coast. As 'bushies', we love to get to the beach for a couple of weeks and take our four boys aged nine to seventeen along with us.

As we were sitting drinking our coffee, I looked over the road and suddenly saw both of our older teenage boys sneaking into the bottle-shop! When I leaped up to 'deal with them', my husband rose, too, and with an unfamiliar firmness said, 'I'll deal with this'. I was so stunned, the best I could offer was a feeble protest. I sat back down and watched him go!

I should explain here that for many years Joe has been the 'quiet achiever', supporting the family. But in the interpersonal department – handling the boys – I was always the one who did the parenting. Sometimes I found this easy, but sometimes very hard.

I knew that Joe had just finished reading your book, *Manhood*, which I'd brought along on the holiday to read. I wondered if this had something to do with his sudden change of behaviour. When he returned from sorting out the boys, I asked him how he had found the book. (Hoping of course he'd learnt all the lessons I intended him to!) His words still ring in my ears. 'Well, mostly I realise I've allowed you to come between the boys and me, and I no longer plan to allow that to happen!'

My second reaction (my first was 'Shit, oh shit, that's not what you were supposed to learn!') was to defend my actions! But almost as soon as I started, I knew he was right. In my efforts to raise these boys to be the sort of men I imagined they should be, I had endeavoured to protect them from what I thought would harm them. Sadly, I think seventeen years ago I was right, but what I had failed to acknowledge and trust was that their dad had grown to be the type of man I wanted them to be – and I hadn't noticed. What a sobering moment.

As I've integrated this learning, I've shared it with other women too. I now believe it's the gap many strong women fall into. We convince ourselves we are a vital bridge between our husbands and sons, when in fact we have become a barrier.

This has given me the confidence to stand back and allow their relationships to develop, and develop they have. Our younger boys have especially benefited. I now allow Joe to intervene when we hit the 'you can't make me do it' wall, and continue to be astounded at how effective his intervention is. Not only has this allowed Joe's relationship with the boys to grow, but also a much more mutual respect between us as to what we both offer as parents.

It hasn't been easy for me to stand back, and under pressure I often still revert to old behaviour. The difference is that Joe's confidence has grown with practice and he stands up to me!

IN A NUTSHELL

- Giving birth to a boy brings to the surface how you feel about males in general. Be careful not to land too many prejudices onto this innocent little boy.
- If you aren't experienced with males (such as through growing up with brothers) then ask men to tell you what it's like being male. Don't be afraid of little boys' bodies!
- Little boys learn love from their mothers. Be kind and warm, and enjoy them.
- Teach your boy about girls and how to get along well with them.
- Praise your son's looks and conversation so he feels good about himself.
- Adjust your parenting as your son gets older. Keep a close eye on safety and the healthy balance of his life, stepping back more as he gets into his teens, but never losing contact with his world, his concerns and whether he is getting out of his depth.
- In adolescence, let him learn from the consequences of his actions (or inactions), such as being late for school if he dawdles. This is the age for learning more about responsibility.
- Encourage an affinity with food preparation from an early age, then enjoy the results. Being of service is the key to lifelong self-esteem.
- Take care not to have big fights in adolescence, especially if you are a single mother. Calm down, then return to the issue logically.
- If you are a strong, capable kind of mum, then be careful that you don't prevent your husband from being close to the kids or doing his part of the parenting. You and your boys need him involved. Encourage your sons and their father to grow close.

Chapter 7

Developing a Healthy Sexuality

We all want our boys to feel good about their sexuality and be able to enjoy it in an intimate, loving and joyful way. But we also want them to be wide awake to the hazards that can accompany sex if it isn't approached with care. Added to the perennial risks of unwanted pregnancy, having enthusiastic consent, and problems with alcohol all add to the mix. These are very good reasons to want our sons to not take their brains off along with their clothes!

Love is powerful and often very confusing. The simplest and most helpful thing young people need to understand is that there are three kinds of attraction:

LIKING – is a mental spark, shared beliefs and preferences, and the spark of another mind.

LOVING – is tender, warm and melting, a heartfelt emotion. It has a sacred kind of dimension.

LUSTING – is spicy, hot, hungry, aching, tingling – need we go on?

Young love is a lot to do with sorting out which is which. Mistakes are inevitable; the trick is to go slowly enough to be able to discover if the attraction has more than one dimension. Parents can help by keeping the brakes on just enough to allow a young person some thinking space. If teenagers are insecure or can't talk to adults about

their choices, they may easily be rushed ahead of their own inner feelings. It's not about stopping young love, but helping a young person be in charge when outside pressures, and their own body, might be rushing them along. The huge sexualisation of our world by the corporate media, through television, music videos, the internet, billboards and magazines, often exerts a pressure on young people to be sexual when they don't really feel ready. Happy relationships are the ones that take time to grow.

Teenagers (and other slow learners!) fall in love quickly. In adolescence we are often so hungry to be in love that we colour anyone who seems a likely candidate in the bright hues of our imagination. We are 'in love with love' as much as with the actual person. In time, the real person shows through and the fantasy meets the reality – which could be good, as real people are much more interesting. Or it could be bad – but at least you've found out!

STORIES FROM THE HEART

WHEN SEX GOES WRONG: THE CREEP FACTOR

In a suburban car dealership, three of the senior men crowd into the small office and close the door. The eighteen-year-old receptionist looks up nervously, because this has happened before. The men surround her and begin to make comments on her clothes and enquire, in coarse language, about her sex life. When they finally leave, she collapses in tears.

A young man, a university student, posts a story on the internet which describes a fantasy about how he captures, sexually assaults and then kills a young woman. The police are tipped off and question the young man, but are unsure how to proceed.

A group of male medical students share a large accommodation facility. They keep a checklist on the kitchen door of the names of the nurses working in a nearby nursing home, and tick them off when someone has managed to 'score' with one of them.

All these men are acting like creeps. 'Creep' is the word we have given to people who act sexually with no feeling for others. They see women as objects. Around someone acting like this, your skin actually does creep, you shrink away.

You'd hope that creepiness was rare, yet creepy attitudes are widespread among teenage boys and men in some settings. Workers with boys and young men have found that while real psychopaths are rare, often peer pressure creates a culture of talking and sometimes behaving towards women that creates a kind of group madness among otherwise normal males. A locker-room mentality develops, whereas individually most of these boys are considerate of and respectful to the women they know. The talk is just a macho pose, but it can shape attitudes and lead to behaviour that gets out of control.

Getting sexuality out into the open, talking about its choices, its values and its responsibilities, shouldn't be neglected with boys.

Through warm and yet definite statements about right and wrong, mothers, fathers and mentors can avoid disaster. Telling our kids – boys and girls – that it's never right to harm others with sex, and also that sex is so much better when it's happy, loving, and equal, will help.

If you act this way yourself, it's half the story. If you talk about why, that is the other half. Talk to your son clearly about the core rule of relationships: never intentionally harm or misuse somebody else. Mums and dads need to share with their sons around the age of ten, before puberty really gets started, about how great love is, physically and in every other way, and that they are going to enjoy it a lot. That it's powerful stuff, and needs to be handled with care, and always with respect for the other person.

The Essential Goodness of Sex

We want our boys to feel good about being male and about being sexual. But very negative messages come flooding in from the media, especially the news media. A teenager may see news about rape in war-torn places, or paedophiles in the church. He may read about horrific sex crimes in the paper. For pre-adolescent boys, the messages that such reports convey about sex must be very unsettling. By thirteen or fourteen most boys have strong sexual feelings and a fascination with the images of women that are presented all around them. Their own sexual urges are really waking up. Boys at this age masturbate at least once a day.[1] Yet nothing positive is being done to honour this new part of their life. It's often not even discussed. As a result, boys are full of doubts. They wonder if a girl will ever be interested in them, if their intentions are honourable, or if they are perverted or bad for feeling the way they do.

Sexual learning includes two parts: the physical details of lovemaking and the much bigger questions of attitudes and values. The practical aspects of sex should be covered in conversations and

explanations with your children from toddlerhood onwards. The really potent information about sex is the attitude you take to it. This has to come from parents and the adult community. If you don't talk about sex (and right and wrong), boys will take their values from friends, television and the internet. Be clear with your boys that there is good sex (respectful, happy, close, careful about pregnancy or HIV/AIDS) and bad sex (using others selfishly).

How People Get Hurt when Sex Isn't Honoured

In my high-school class (like every high-school class since the beginning of time!) there was a girl whose breasts grew larger and earlier than the other girls. Two boys in the class, who were a little older than the others, would sit at the back and catcall crudely every time Jeannie walked into the classroom. Jeannie was quite outgoing up until this time, but you could see her confidence trickle away – they made her life miserable. Nobody liked this, but nobody did anything about it. I wished we had had a strong enough boy-culture to tackle them, to tell them to stop.

In another instance, a good friend of mine at school, Joseph, was Maltese. Perhaps because he was a bit short, or just because he was a migrant, some of the boys took to calling him a 'poofter', and made a game of ducking away from him in the playground. It didn't seem malicious in intent, but it went on too long and too often. Joe became more and more of an outsider, and eventually quit school. When I look back on those times, I feel regret and shame at not speaking up.

Talk to your kids about sexual bullying at their school, and how or if it happens. Discuss how they could intervene. When they use derogatory words or insults casually themselves, about girls or other sexualities, confront them about it.

A lot of boys' 'creep' behaviour is mainly due to ignorance or thoughtlessness – it isn't really sinister. Adults or wiser boys need to simply say something casual but clear-cut – and stop the abuse. Younger boys will take their cues from older ones or from men, and the practice will stop. Boy-culture is just the blind leading the blind so much of the time, and easily sinks to the lowest denominator. Robert Bly calls it a 'sibling society' with no elders.[2]

Peer pressure can work for good as well as bad. Several times in my youth I and other friends were in situations where we prevented rapes from taking place. Vietnam vets have told me about how, during the course of that war, they talked comrades out of committing atrocities when overcome with grief or anger. The infamous My Lai massacre of 1968 was stopped by other US soldiers landing in helicopters to confront the murderers, saving possibly hundreds more innocents being killed. Keeping each other out of trouble is a big part of how men help each other.

It takes skill to steer things in a better direction in a group situation. Kids can only learn these skills if they have seen someone else handling a similar situation well. When I worked in schools, I often noticed that if a child was hurt accidentally in sport, one of the bigger boys would be very caring and helpful. At other times, though, where there was no boy with these qualities present, the group would just laugh and add humiliation to injury, or be awkward and look away if a smaller boy was really distressed. The boys who helped often came from large families where they had kid sisters and brothers and, I guess, were used to taking a nurturing role. They were more rounded human beings, and good to have around.

Someone to Talk To

A big problem for many boys is the difficulty they have in talking about personal matters with their friends. In my boyhood, no discussion ever seemed to go deeper than last night's episode of *Mission Impossible*. Girls, on the other hand, talked things through endlessly. There were many problems we boys could have talked over. The boy I sat next to in class was often beaten up by his alcoholic father. Another's parents divorced messily during the final year. I only learnt of these things many years later, yet I spent thousands of hours with these boys. Three of my school friends took their own lives, either during or in the few years following school. (In fact, school is preventive of suicide, and the rate rises dramatically once boys leave school, indicating that the friendship and support structures of school are a big plus.)

If parents – especially dads, uncles and grandfathers, as well as mothers – talk to their boys openly and listen to their problems, there is a better chance that the boys will carry these skills into their peer group. What a difference that would make.

How Boys Feel about Girls

Boys in their mid-teens think that girls are wonderful. They envy the easy way girls laugh and talk with their friends, their 'savvy' and their physical grace. But, above all, they are aware of girls' tantalising sexual promise. Added to this heady brew is a strong romantic streak that many boys have. They can inject a real spiritual intensity into idealising a particular girl as the epitome of everything noble and pure.

But something gets in the way of everyday relating to real girls. Girls make conversation more easily than boys. It's hard for boys to know what to say to them. And in high school, the girls are much more mature physically than the boys of the same age. They appear like goddesses to the boys, who are mostly still runts with hollow chests and short legs!

Girls seem to hold all the cards. Many boys (especially the non-athletic, the ill-clad, and those with big noses or fat or skinny legs) begin to think they aren't ever going to make it with a girl. They feel destined to be losers in the romantic stakes. This sits very heavily on their minds.

Of course, unknown to the boys, the girls too are often feeling uncertain and awkward. They would actually like to talk, mix and share affection with the boys. If the boys were a little more socially skilled or bolder, many more affirming things could happen between

the genders. Instead, the girls whisper to each other and mock the boys, the boys harass and rubbish the girls, and the quiet ones stand back from it all and just brood.

For most kids, this is just depressing and sad. Eventually some confidence develops and things improve. But for some young men, an exploitive mentality often sets in, an 'if I

can't meet girls as equals, I'll have to control them'. This isn't helped by the phenomenon of degrading internet porn, or just everyday MTV music clips that use girls as 'eye candy' to sell songs. Showing someone something they can't have is cruel and abusive. Deep down, this feeds a strong, sexually charged and understandable anger in boys if they don't get much chance to talk and engage with real girls, or experience respect and liking from them. Their attitude to women and their ability to relate to girls as people just gets worse.

Today both men and women share an anger at the use of images in advertising which grab our sons by the penis, so to speak. A young man's heart is not unconnected from his pelvis but, as one young man wrote, 'the pictures never love you back'.

A great many men carry from boyhood a huge inferiority complex in the area of sex and romance. It makes them poor lovers, and their wives may soon lose interest. This makes the men desperate for sex; being desperate makes them unlovable; and being unlovable makes them desperate all over again. This may well be the cause of many marriage break-ups. Boyhood is the time when some positive words, some affection and some honour from parents and friends can make a boy brave and self-believing enough to be a good sexual partner for life.

How Boys Shut Down Their Bodies

Have you noticed the way that boys begin shutting down their feelings once they reach school age? Little boys are full of feelings and energies. But in the jungle of the schoolyard they soon grow ashamed of useful and healthy emotions like sadness, fear or tenderness. To make himself cope, a boy suppresses his feelings and tenses his body. If you touch the shoulders of a ten-year-old boy, you will often find that his muscles are rock-hard with tension.

Then, one day, puberty strikes. The boy is suddenly aware of a wonderful feeling of 'aliveness', of quickening – all located in the one place! It's no wonder that a boy soon attaches all his feelings of closeness (and all his sense of aliveness and wellbeing) to the activities of his penis.

Boys want to feel alive in their bodies. That's why they like music with a heavy beat, and why they love activity, speed and danger. They instinctively know this can help them break through into manhood. A boy who enjoys his body and can hug his mum, dad and sisters often has many ways to feel good – dancing, drumming, or playing sport for the buzz of the game itself. For these boys, sex carries a little less weight – it's a pleasure rather than an obsession.

Keeping Things Open and Positive

Parents must be careful not to drive sexuality underground by ridiculing their son about sex or girls. Do talk about it when it comes up in movies or on the television or in discussions at the table. As boys pass the age of ten, use sexual words casually and normally in conversation – 'masturbation', 'lovemaking', 'orgasm', as well as the darker ones, such as 'rape' and 'incest'. They need to know that you know about these aspects of life. But especially be more open about sex as a lovely and exciting aspect of life.

Demand maturity – with good humour. If you notice your sons sniggering or reacting in a silly way to an incident on the television in the conversation, don't just let it go – ask them about it and fill out their understanding. But end with a joke or a laugh – give things a positive spin. The antidote to creepiness is an infusion of warmth, humour and openness.

Mothers can really help here. If a mother is affectionate, praises her son's attractiveness (without flirting with him), and if his father shows respect for the mother and is warm and affectionate to her,

then the boy learns how to relate to girls with attraction and *equality*. If boys and girls are encouraged in school or youth groups to talk and mix and have friendships that are not 'dates', they can learn more about the opposite sex without the self-consciousness of 'going steady'. They can graduate in friendship first and major in romance later.

PRACTICAL HELP

BOYS WHO WANT TO BE GIRLS

Often parents will ask about a son who from a young age likes dressing up as a girl, prefers the company of girls or enjoys activities normally associated with girls. My advice, and that of most psychologists worldwide, is that our children thrive best when we accept them as they are. A little boy wanting to dress as a girl does not necessarily mean that he is transgender or gay. Only about a fifth of boys who like girls' clothes as children turn out to be transgender, and many transgender teens do not show any signs during childhood.[3] So the best thing is to wait and see.

Still, by early or mid-teens, some boys have strong feelings of being 'born in the wrong body' and express a desire to change sex. The research suggests that this is a real and important signal about who they feel they are, and that they should be supported in exploring this option.[4] Denying or trying to suppress such feelings at this age can lead to severe depression, suicidal thoughts or other harmful behaviour. Thankfully, most countries now have clinics and counselling services in hospitals which specialise in this area and your doctor can put you in touch with them.

It's a big thing to take powerful hormones or contemplate surgical changes to the body you were born with, and so it's really important to get good information, and go calmly and slowly. Every boy's choices and needs will differ. After taking all the information on board and weighing up the pros and cons, boys who wish to change gender may be offered hormones to delay puberty so that their bodies don't develop features that will cause them more distress, such as facial hair or a deeper voice. This also buys them time in order to develop the maturity and life experience they need to decide if they wish to go further. Then, at around eighteen, they may be offered hormones to begin to change the appearance of their body as much as possible. And if this is still not enough, they can investigate the option of surgery to approach a more female body type.

It's a difficult question for parents, because compared to simply dressing as the opposite sex, having your body changed by surgery is largely irreversible, and one never in reality changes gender, just the outer aspects. And powerful hormones are not without risks. Some feminist writers are making a case that if we did not have such a gendered world – where all boys felt they had to be a certain kind of masculine and girls a certain kind of feminine, then everyone – especially kids who feel differently – could just be themselves and find their own style and role. Without harming or taking risks with their body.

The research on whether 'transitioning' makes young people happier long term, is cautiously positive. Tavistock and Portman – the leading clinic in the UK – has said that 'we are building the data as we go',[5] and that is an honest appraisal. Care is needed. People who go back on the decision – and de-transition, as best they can, are not always reported in studies. Decisions we make as teenagers are so often the result of turmoil and the process of finding who we are, and those things change. Nonetheless, the balance of studies seems to be that most transgender people are happier to have changed than not.[6] It's still not easy being a transitioned person, but for most, it's better than being not able to.

There are gradations; some people transition without having genital surgery, as that is the most irreversible step of all. Some try the hormones, and then stop in their later teens or twenties and return to their original selves. I hope that the world changes quickly to be a place where we don't think in rigid terms of what constitutes a boy or a girl, man or woman, so that being in-between or different altogether is just fine. Perhaps this might make more kids able to just be themselves.

A 2009 Home Office study estimated that there are 300,000 to 500,000 transgender people in the UK.[7]

Your Son and Online Porn

When we were teenagers, serious pornography was almost unheard of. Of course, most boys managed to garner a small stash of magazines showing almost-nude young women, who were usually referred to in the magazines as 'co-eds', possibly to emphasise their educational status. Otherwise, the poster of Raquel Welch in a rabbit skin bikini (made from just two rabbits!) from the film *One Million Years B.C.* graced some bedroom walls, and that was it. Parents either didn't notice or didn't think it worth commenting on.

As a psychologist I would have regarded this – the boys' interest and their parents' non-interference – as healthy and normal, as long as it was discreet and private, like sex itself. Respectful boundaries are important in how we treat each other, especially in those parts of life that involve emotional closeness and vulnerability.

The rise of online pornography has blown all this out of the water. Today's mental-health professionals are struggling to find a balanced reaction between being sex-positive, and yet cautioning about the very real harms of ongoing exposure. Kids will see porn, sadly often at young ages, and need us to talk about it with them. But its worsening nature, and addictive qualities, are increasing concern worldwide.

In 2012, the renowned Tavistock Clinic in London sounded an alarm about the rise in cases of young boys experiencing addiction to hard-core porn online. One boy who had started using porn at ten years of age told a counsellor, 'I didn't know it was possible for people to do those sort of things. The websites led me to other websites, and soon I was looking at weirder stuff I could never have imagined – animals, children, stabbing and strangling.' For three years, unknown to his parents, this boy viewed porn for hours every night. He is still deeply disturbed by its effects on him. He told the counsellor, 'It still makes me think I might never have a proper girlfriend – the pictures still come back to me sometimes. It makes me want to shout "Stop, stop!"'[8]

Online porn addiction has spilled over into rapes and assaults in the real world. Among the Tavistock's patients was a thirteen-year-old who was found to have been abusing his five-year-old sister. A twelve-year-old was exposing himself to teachers and other students at school.

A UK parliamentary report in 2012 found that 80 per cent of sixteen-year-old boys regularly access porn online. And one in three ten-year-olds has seen explicit material.[9] It's these younger boys who are the most concern, because their sexuality is still being formed and can easily be moulded towards cruelty and non-intimate sex. One does have to ask, what were these boys' parents doing – didn't they know about their sons' online behaviour?

Researchers have found that the more that porn is viewed by boys or men, the more those males denigrate and dehumanise women – they lose respect for them as people. And they see them as deserving of maltreatment.[10] Also, the nature of solitary sexuality has changed: what once satisfied is now not enough, and the viewer seeks stronger material. Porn sites are designed to entrap, sometimes even using children's cartoon characters or placement among game sites to get children to click through.

Neuropsychologist Susan Greenfield has written extensively about how the internet shapes brains and makes instant gratification an addiction in itself.[11] Boys who get addicted to online porn often spend hours a day trawling the net when they are supposed to be asleep or doing their homework. Many tell counsellors they now find real girls too difficult to relate to – they prefer 'sex' online.

Given the proliferation of smartphones and wireless devices with internet connections, your son is likely to be shown things by friends. Difficult as you may find it, it's important to talk calmly and reasonably about this: that there is weird pornography about, that it's harmful to keep looking at, and that you want him not to do that. (It's ongoing exposure that you really want to prevent.) Have filters on your computer(s), and only have computer access in public parts of your house, not in bedrooms. If your kids have smartphones, don't let them keep them overnight – leave them all on chargers in the kitchen. Don't make your son feel bad for being curious about or attracted to pictures of women – that's totally normal. But explain that you do want to guard him against getting addicted. Porn is very tempting, and some of his peers will probably urge him to 'look at this'. A boy who can say, 'no thanks, that stuff messes with your head', is going to be the one who finds that his real-life relationships are a whole lot better and happier.

Finally, just as we have laws to restrict kids' access to other harmful things, like alcohol and tobacco, making internet service providers restrict pornography, so that it can't be accessed without deliberate and identified actions, is essential. Pornography is a bigger industry than sport, worth billions of dollars, so it's a powerful lobby group. Taming it will take some real resolve.

Countering the Effects of Porn

A very experienced counsellor, Elizabeth Clark, has pinpointed how pornography teaches boys some serious misinformation, which will make sex go badly for them if we don't help them get it straight. In her book *Love, Sex and No Regrets for Today's Teens*,[12] she explains that pornography contains six damaging myths.

1. *Sex is anonymous.* In porn it doesn't matter if you are attracted to the other person or them to you. It is best if the person is not real to you, has no feelings, family, cares, soul, future or physical limits.
2. *Sex is fast.* In porn, there is no kissing or caressing, no unfolding, no allowing arousal to get the body ready.
3. *Sex is disconnected.* In porn, no eyes meet. Bodies are not usually positioned facing one another. There are no smiles or moments when soul meets soul, friend meets friend, lover meets lover. Because it doesn't matter who is entering you.
4. *Sex degrades women but that's OK.* They are pummelled, slapped and choked, they are mocked and discarded. They are assumed stupid and without worth. But the important message of porn is that this does not matter because women love this degradation and abuse. It turns them on. It is all part of the fun. (In porn it's almost never the man who is hurt or humiliated.)

5. *Women are always ready.* Sexy girls are always ready for sex, anytime, any place with anyone and in any way. They just want sex all the time. Their bodies require no time or touch, and no relationship.

6. *Porn sex is a blast.* At the end of the film everyone has had a great time. Everyone is happy and satisfied, and content.

If your son believes any of these, then he will have terrible encounters with girls. The reason is that happy sex is the complete opposite – it's personal, it takes time, there is lots of connection, and the girl and boy both treat each other kindly. He would want to be treated kindly or well, so point out to him the simple human fact that you give what you would want to receive. Timing and readiness are what makes lovemaking good. And when it's good, it's wonderful. Our heart, mind and body are not split, and so all our parts are along for the ride. Once you've experience that, you won't settle for less.

Start by asking your son – Do you want to be able to have happy sex with a girl who loves you back? Then you have to start to learn. And being emotionally vulnerable and taking risks in love are a part of that.

What If Your Son Is Gay?

Psychologists have made a remarkable observation of our inner world: most of us imagine a fantasy family long before we have a real one.[13] We picture a 'dream family' that we expect our family to eventually look and behave like. Even before our children are born, we have their lives mapped out for them! And what conservative dreams they usually are – a rewarding career, a happy marriage, and grandchildren to sit on our knee! When our real family comes along, we all unconsciously try to make it conform to our fond hopes and dreams.

Finding out that your teenage son is gay rewrites the imagined future you may have mapped out for him. Some grief is natural and OK. But when it's all boiled down, the concerns of parents of a gay son are just the same as those of any parent. You want your son to have a happy life. You hope that he will handle his sexuality in a responsible and self-respecting way. And you hope that he will not move into worlds that are beyond your reach or understanding.

Teenage LGBTI children need our support. There is no doubt they are at risk – from our rejection and from a harsh world. It's clear that many youth suicides are caused by youngsters discovering they are gay.[14] Gay kids need parents who will listen and understand, and protect them from harassment or persecution. They also need role models. If your church, extended family, sporting group or circle of friends includes happily gay men or lesbian women, then it's a huge plus.

The evidence is mounting that some babies are born with certain hormonal settings from early in the womb, which may set the brain as either gay, bisexual or heterosexual (at least one in ten young men are in the first two categories).[15] If you love and support your son, he will be more likely to be self-respecting and careful about safe sex. There are countless happy and successful gay men and women. Talking to other parents of gay offspring is the very best thing you can do. (Groups such as PFLAG – Parents and Friends of Lesbians and Gays – exist worldwide and offer support.) A gay son can take you into a world of interesting and wonderful people!

Computer Games

Most parents are concerned about computer gaming and their son – how much to allow, which games, and who they are playing with. And they should be – it's a slack parent who is happy that the kid is occupied and quiet in their room for days at a stretch, who just says, 'well, what can you do?' No book on boys would be complete without addressing this, so here goes.

First the big picture. According to a Pew Centre study, 'Boys are significantly more likely to play games daily than girls, with 39 per cent of boys reporting daily game play and 22 per cent of girls reporting the same.'[16]

They do it for fun and relaxation. And everyone needs fun and relaxation in their lives. Games don't teach you a lot – except how to play more games – but that's not their purpose. They are good – to a point – for letting off steam and escaping life when it's all a bit too hard. You can be a hero, a winner. You can kill zombies! And we all need to do a bit of that.

Also, gaming is increasingly social. Boys play games together with other friends at each other's houses, or networked online. Today they can even talk as they play. They also play with people in other countries, including complete strangers. But for the most part, its among friends, and is part of being socially connected that translates to the real world, just like an interest in sport or movies or science fiction or music. Those are the plusses.

The negatives depend a lot on the child. The American Psychiatric Association has now recognised a diagnosis, still tentative but likely to be ratified, of Internet Gaming Disorder (in other words, addiction).[17] It affects up to 5 per cent of gamer children and adults. The main symptoms are those that fit any addiction.

1. It becomes an obsession.
2. They are anxious and very unhappy when it's not available.
3. They do it more and more, and need it more and more, as time goes on.
4. They lose interest in and participation in other activities that previously enhanced their life.
5. They become deceptive and sneaky about their use.
6. They use it to manage anxiety and stress rather than deal with the causes.

Lots of parents will recognise some of those, but if you have all six, it's probably a concern. In my experience, serious problems with computer gaming usually arise in kids whose lives are not going well for other reasons – they are under a lot of stress (and anxiety problems are now epidemic in teenage school children). Or they have poor social skills – including kids on the autistic spectrum for whom the real social world can be very difficult to navigate. They don't enjoy sport or other activities (music, hobbies, creative arts, nature) much or nobody has encouraged or supported them to take these up. And to me the most important one – they haven't got adults interested in doing things with them. And also, in a family, everyone should be helping make the meals, do the laundry, garden, and look after pets, and not even have hours to hunker away in darkened bedrooms.

So, what to do? The answers then are probably on two main streams – some stick, and some carrot, if you like.

Putting the Brakes On

Left to themselves, most boys' gaming will get out of control. Kids are not good at putting limits on themselves, because of their immature brain development, and one of our jobs as parent is to provide these limits.

Most parents I have talked to around the world are doing two simple things. They have limits – 30 or 40 minutes a night, and two hours on the weekend is common. Some special times when friends come over and play for a few hours from time to time. But don't feel you have to be like other families – you decide what works best for your own values, and your own kids.

It's much better to have a gaming time allocation clearly defined than to be for ever bickering or nagging about vague ideas of 'you've been on that computer too much'. Though of course some monitoring is still going to be needed.

Many families now have opted for the whole family going offline – usually at dinner time, and the phones and devices go on to chargers. They don't have screens in bedrooms (remember the pornography concern here as well). In many homes now, the internet goes off at night, and people find they are much more relaxed and, even more importantly, connect better with each other.[18]

Having More Good Things to Do

Researchers say it's not that gaming is harmful itself, but its effect on sleep, obesity, etc., is the 'opportunity cost' – the time gaming takes up in boys' lives so they miss out on other things.[19] Exercise is an obvious one – school-aged kids need to be outside and doing more than moving their thumbs. School itself has become more sedentary, so after school is the best chance to be physically active. Socialising with family, and friends, and brothers and sisters. Families can have almost no conversations if a boy is gaming in his room for hours a night. It doesn't hurt to occasionally play the games with them, know what kind of games they play (be strong on ratings too, there are dire games around – including games involving rape or killing women just 'for fun'). And the research is now very clear that gaming DOES increase violent behaviour, especially in kids who are vulnerable or disposed already (for example, if they have experienced family violence, been bullied, or lack social skills and feel isolated).[20]

If your family life is relaxed but active you do other things with your kids that keep them physical, sociable, out in nature. You get together with folks of all ages, and they can meet the opposite sex (or same sex) in safe settings of your friends and extended family, then they will find their feet in the big world.

And see that real life is a good place that they don't need to retreat from, at least not all the time!

IN A NUTSHELL

- Teach boys about the difference between liking, loving and lusting. All are OK, but you shouldn't mix them up.
- Have a small rite of passage when he enters double figures (i.e. reaches age ten) and give him some positive messages about sex.
- Guard against creepiness by teaching your son to be respectful of all people. Help him to find settings and activities where he can get to know girls as friends.
- Discourage the trend to sexualise boy–girl relationships under sixteen years of age.
- Remember that boys, too, want to be loved, not just 'sexed'. Affirm and support their romantic side.
- Help them keep their bodies alive through dance, drumming, music, massage and so on. Continue to hug and show affection to your sons as long as they are comfortable with it.
- Tenderness is learnt by receiving it – from babyhood onwards. The real lessons about relationships are learnt by age three.
- Masturbation isn't just harmless, it's good for you.
- Discourage pornography dependence; but discuss it and its messages openly. Don't shame a boy for his interest, but talk about what good erotica is – i.e. respectful, happy, and involving relationships.
- Mothers can help sons understand what girls like in young men – kindness, conversation and a sense of fun.
- Not all boys are straight. One in ten might have a different sexuality and need help and support to grow into that.

Chapter 8

Out into the Big World

To Nursery, or Not?

In the tender early part of his life, your boy is raised at home and among your friends and extended family. But in the modern world, that has to change (unless you are living a fairly alternative lifestyle). Sooner or later, your boy will move into environments that may be less kind, and also less boy-friendly or boy-aware. (I've spent thirty years educating teachers and childcare professionals about boys' needs, but it's still very early days.)

The first big decision for many parents of boys is whether to use childcare or nursery. There is huge pressure in society today, financial, and social, for both parents, dads and mums, to work, full-time if possible. Politicians and employers don't see any problem with very young children being in institutional care and not with their families, as if all they need is minding. Of course, today this is very much spun as 'early learning', as if it's actually better than what a loving parent can provide. (The titles match the anxieties of the time – it was 'minding' in the nineteenth century when you just needed to know they would be there and still alive at the end of the day. Then 'care' when our anxieties were about warmth and lovingness. 'Nursery', of course, has that reassuring Mary Poppins vibe that calms British sensibilities. And now, 'early learning', when we care more than anything else about competitive advantage.)

Now, there *are* some kids who are better off out of the home for part of each day – if their caregiver is drug-addicted, severely depressed, abusive, or homeless or their environment bleak and deprived. But in my experience, the average child with an attentive and caring mother, father or grandparent (which was for centuries the tradition) will have a more responsive, attuned and interesting time just going about their daily life than even the richest group situation can offer. We put ourselves down when we think we are not educators. One worker told me (and she was very high-ranking in the industry), that 'early learning just means there are letters painted on the blocks'.

It's not that nursery or daycare is not an important provision – in fact it is a right, hard-won and important to always have available. It's not that it's not a vital part of gender equality that women have as much right to be in the workforce, as well as being parents, as men do. It's not that most daycare staff are not warm, skilful and incredibly dedicated to trying to meet the individual needs of each child. It's just that it can't possibly match one to one care on the frequency and attunement of interaction. Sheer economics mean that staff ratios don't come close to allowing the amount of time that a parent can provide. This matters less as a child gets older, and by three or four, part-time group care – essentially, pre-school – can of course be a plus.

There are two things to remember. Firstly, kids differ. Some kids find daycare or nursery fun, or at least harmless, but some find it acutely stressful. And in boys, that generally shows as aggression rather than grief. They just start to distance themselves and shut down. Girls learn to compete for attention and become adroit social animals but also lessen their vulnerability to getting too trusting, too close to either staff or other children.

There is a lot of research that you can read on this. I wrote a whole book summing it up called *Raising Babies – Should Under 3s Go to Nursery?*[1] In essence the message is that some kids are not affected a great deal and others are. That it's dose-related, so the later you start, the less time you go for, and the better the quality – with caring, well-paid, and stable long-term staff, the better. It isn't all bad, used at the right age, and in the right way, and if it's a necessity for family survival.

But secondly, the concerns voiced by neurobiologist Alan Schore, cited earlier, indicate that probably no boys under the age of one should be in group care. And since that doesn't immediately change the moment they turn one, it is still less desirable in their second year, and still second-rate to what we can provide in their third. Girls are somewhat more resilient to the way their attachment bonds are stretched by periods of time away from mum or dad or grandparent, if that is their main carer. But that too depends on the girl.

I don't think the important studies have actually been done. What if long hours spent in group care correlate with having marital problems as an adult, due to difficulties in attunement or trust? What if they affect our ability to be a parent ourselves, when that time comes. What if the effects are not in reading ability in grade two or behaviour at seven, but are deeper and more long-term?

With the massive increase in adolescent stress and depression that we are seeing, especially in the US where most kids are in daycare by the age of one, I sincerely hope that none of these turns out to be the case. I am just saying that I don't think we know. For 300,000 years, kids were raised by half a dozen adults who loved them. The same ones from birth to adulthood. And we mess with that at our peril.

Boys and School

Many schools today are a battleground. Teachers are overstressed and underpaid; kids have less and less socialisation from home (good manners, calm influences, feeling wanted and loved). The number of men in schools has plummeted; more and more it is women who have to front up to physically intimidating and disrespectful boys. The classroom becomes a battle for survival with only two goals – getting the girls to achieve and getting the boys to behave.

So boys create stress, but they themselves are suffering, too. Girls outperform boys in almost every subject area. Something has to be done about boys' motivation, for everyone's sake.

From what we have already described here about brain differences, hormones and the need for male role models, it's clear that schools can and must change if they are to become good places for boys. Here are some starting points:

1. A Later Starting Age for Boys?

While the subject of brain differences is a controversial one, there is one difference nobody disputes – that boys develop more slowly than girls. And that has a massive implication for starting school.

At the age of five, when UK and Australian children start serious schooling, boys' brains are an astonishing six to twelve months less developed than girls'. They are especially delayed in fine-motor skills, which is the ability to control their fingers and hold a pen or scissors. And since they are still in the stage of gross-motor development, developing the nerves to their bigger arm, leg and body muscles, they will be itching to move their bodies around – so they will not be good at sitting still. (Girls do it in reverse: their brains go

PRACTICAL HELP

KNOWING WHEN TO START

All children should attend kindergarten or half-day pre-school from around four years of age, since they need the social stimulation and wider experiences it provides (and because parents need a break!). Pre-school has fully trained teachers who provide playful but appropriate learning experiences that are a halfway step to school.

In pre-school or kindergarten, it will become clear which boys are ready for more formal learning – they are happy to sit and do work in books or craft, and are able to talk happily – and which boys are still needing to run about, and are not yet good with a crayon or pencil.

From your own observations, discussion with the pre-school teacher, and perhaps checking out what is expected of children going into primary school, you will soon get an idea – ready, or not ready yet. If it's possible to take another year in a less formal environment, your boy will have a whole year more to get ready to do really well in more formal education. Sitting still at a desk is often hard and painful for small boys. In early primary school, boys (whose motor nerves are still growing) actually get signals from their body saying, 'Move around. Use me.' To a stressed-out Grade 1 teacher, this looks like misbehaviour.

A boy sees that his craft work, drawing and writing are not as good as the girls', and thinks, 'this is not for me!'. He quickly switches off from learning – especially if there is not a male teacher anywhere in sight to give that sense that learning is a male thing, too. 'School is for girls', he tells himself.

There is much more that we can do to make school boy-friendly. But the first question – is he ready yet? – is perhaps the most important place to start.

straight to finger coordination, and they often need help in body strengthening by bouncing on trampolines and playing basketball or swimming.)[2]

The other delay boys experience is in using words well. This affects being able to tell a teacher what they need, answer questions in class, and communicate with other children. Many boys at five are still immature socially, and not really ready for the demands of a more formal school environment. In talking to early childhood teachers the same message comes through: many boys should wait another year.

In fact the calendar is a terrible way of deciding who should start school. Kids vary so much, and with a once-a-year intake some will always be young for their year. Studies from the UK show that kids who are young for their year often do worse right through school.[3] It's important to treat every child as an individual case and to think about each, not in terms of 'how old?', but rather 'how ready?' In boys' cases, the answer is often: not yet.

2. More Men of the Right Kind in Schools

Because of divorce and single motherhood, up to a third of boys have no father present at home.[4] The six-to-fourteen age range is the period when boys most hunger for male encouragement and example. So it's vital we get more men into primary-school teaching. Not just any men – they have to be the right kind of men.

I have asked many teachers to describe the right kind of man to work with boys. Two qualities come up again and again:

1. A mixture of warmth and sternness. Someone who obviously enjoys youngsters and gives praise where it is due. A man who doesn't need to be 'one of the boys', and has a slightly gruff, no-nonsense manner! But he must have warmth and a sense of humour. This means that order prevails, and boys can get on with the class work, excursion, sport or whatever.
2. A lack of defensiveness. A man who is not only in charge, but is so in a way that doesn't issue a challenge to every testosterone-boosted boy in the room. He doesn't need to prove anything and doesn't feel threatened by youthful exuberance.[5]

One wise woman teacher put it like this: 'Every boy who has been expelled while I was at this school did so in the following way. They got into a fight with a male teacher, who sent for another male teacher, who just irritated the boy even more. It became a battle of wills with no room to back down.'

PRACTICAL HELP

HOW TO SPOT AN UNDER–FATHERED BOY IN SCHOOL

There are four main clues that a boy is seriously under-fathered:

1. an aggressive style of relating
2. hyper-masculine behaviour and interests (guns, muscles, trucks – death!)
3. an extremely limited repertoire of behaviour (standing around grunting and being 'cool'), and
4. a derogatory attitude to women, gays and other minorities.

These traits are familiar to every secondary-school teacher in the Western world. Let's examine what is causing them.

The aggressive style of relating is a boy's cover-up for feeling unsure of himself. Lacking praise and respect from older males, he puts on a tough act. The rule is – put down someone else before they put you down. If a boy has little contact with his father or other men, then he doesn't really know how to be a man. He doesn't have the words, the insights into himself or a handle on his feelings. Because he's never seen it done, he doesn't know how to:

- deal with a conflict in a good-humoured way
- talk to women easily and without being sexist, or
- express appreciation or sadness, or to say sorry, and so on.

Anything we can do to put good men into these boys' lives is going to have a life-saving effect down the track.

My memory of boyhood, and that of many men I talk to, is of considerable fear of being ridiculed or being beaten up by other boys. Boys dread ridicule – however tough they act. They often feel deeply ashamed of their slowness with reading aloud or looking dumb in the

classroom. They dread being shown up by a teacher. Boys who are smart have the opposite problem – being called a 'nerd', a 'teacher's pet', and also facing ridicule or exclusion. If you are creative or different, you run the risk of being labelled a 'poofter' – or worse!

The boy with good support from his father and mother, uncles and so on can handle this better because he doesn't feel that his maleness is on trial. But a boy who doesn't feel assured of his masculinity has to cover up. The best protection is to act tough and uncaring, and to radiate aggression, so that nobody thinks you're scared. You get in first and put people down as a matter of course. This way you feel safer.

The same effect takes place with interests. A tough dude has to have tough interests. Boys (not having the perspective of a real man around to broaden their interests with hobbies, sports or music, or to involve them in creative work in a shed or garden) gravitate to those things that make them feel masculine – action figures with huge muscles, guns, trucks, and so on.

PRAISE IS THE ANTIDOTE

If a father, uncle or older friend praises a boy, this automatically widens that boy's self-image. Imagine the family are coming home from a barbecue with friends. The dad says casually, 'You were really good with the little kids, organising that cricket match. They loved it!' The boy drinks this compliment in deep. A male teacher or a friend sees the boy tapping on the table in a complex rhythm: 'You know, you could be a drummer – that's a really hard rhythm.' Each of these comments boosts the boy's sense of himself. He is less dependent on peer approval and more willing to try new things.

WHAT ARE YOU, A GIRL?

If you don't know what you are, there is one way to firm up your self-image – by declaring what you are not. Boys specialist Dr Rex Stoessiger has noticed that boys who don't have a positive male image define themselves by being *not girls*.[6] So they reject in themselves everything that they perceive girls to be – soft, talkative, emotional, cooperative, caring and affectionate. And they are much more likely to show racism too. Neo-Nazi groups are full of young men with father issues. Having someone to hate and reject makes you feel stronger, more worthy. Finding better role models is the key to many current problems – including radicalisation and terrorism. The racists and the terrorists have a lot in common.

A teacher I was talking to recently illustrated the effect of role-modelling beautifully. In the large country high school where she taught, the normally girl-dominated subject of art had recently become a popular choice for boys, because the new art teacher was a man who had a good-hearted personality. He was a father with kids of his own – warm, positive, a bit stern. He had interests that the kids respected. He organised school surfing competitions, was a keen surfer, and liked the outdoors. The result: a sudden upsurge of boys' painting, sculpture and creativity, which lasted several years after this man left the school.

'Being cool' is a subtle thing – for kids are not fooled for long by appearances. When I was in high school, we got a new, young maths teacher, Mr Clayfoote, who wore jeans and an earring (in 1965!) and drove a red Camaro with GT stripes. He enjoyed a brief honeymoon period, surrounded by boys in the school ground and the object of many girlish daydreams. But it soon wore off, because the kids weren't interested in someone who was just interested in being admired. Early in his second term, Mr Clayfoote lost his licence for drink driving, and had to walk to school after that. His role-model status took a bit of a dive.

Discipline Problems Call for Our Involvement

Boys make trouble to get noticed. In schools all around the world where I have consulted, there is a proven equation: an under-fathered boy equals a discipline problem in school. Under-fathered boys unconsciously want men to be involved and to address the problems of their lives, but don't know how to ask. Girls *ask* for help, but boys often just *act* for help. If we get men teachers involved with under-fathered boys (ideally, before they make trouble), we can turn their lives around. And if boys do get into trouble, male teachers should work with them to guide and help them.

Studies have found that boys in school who act as if they don't care really *do* want to be successful and included.[7] We have just made the slope too steep for them. We punish them, but we don't offer leadership. Leadership is not just something that comes from the podium at assembly; it has to be personal.

Too often boys' vitality is seen as a threat, to be squashed. The squashing was once done by caning and by grinding work; now it is done by suspensions, or time-out rooms, or by tedious and bureaucratic 'report' systems. One teacher described to me his school's disciplinary report system as 'lingering, inconclusive and impersonal'. This is all based on a psychology of distance, not closeness: 'If you're bad, we'll isolate you.' It should be: 'If you need help that badly, we'll get involved with you.' School should be a place of affection, involvement and attachment. The more needy the boy is, the more he should receive.

There's no reason why school can't be as affectionate, laughter-filled, warm and nurturing as a good family is, with teachers being long-term 'uncles' and 'aunts' to kids. Boys learn best when they feel cared about, safe and valued.

3. Bullying

It's a sad fact that getting bullied is a part of many boys' lives. A study of 20,000 primary- and secondary-school children across Australia found that one in five students were bullied at school at least once a week.[8] Dr Ken Rigby and Dr Phillip Slee, prominent experts on bullying, believe that schools play a big part in creating the problem and in curing it – but parents can help, too.

Ken Rigby told a conference on the subject that too many classrooms are based on competition, which leads to less able students feeling excluded and resentful. So bullying is a way for some boys of getting back some dignity. Dr Rigby believes that many schools themselves bully their students, belittling them, making them feel useless, not helping them in a dignified way to learn and change.

My experience is that violent bullies are often hit a lot at home, and have lost the natural reluctance that most children have to causing harm to others. They do to others what is done to them. Bullying is part of a bygone era, in which men hit their wives routinely, wives and husbands hit children, and so on. As abusive parenting disappears, bullying will be much less common.

Ken Rigby recommends that while schools need to have rules about bullying (and that sometimes students have to be excluded from school for the protection of others), a whole-school policy is the best solution. This means group discussions and teaching in the classroom about bullying, what it is, and that it is not OK. It also includes having adequate staff in the playground and always intervening actively when children report being bullied. The best methods involve not 'bullying the bully', but working with bullies and the group of children affected so they understand the hurt they are causing, and so make the problem a 'shared concern' of the group.

These approaches are often quite successful. Discussion methods have a big advantage over punishment in that they don't drive the problem underground or escalate it by making the bully more excluded or more of a social failure.

What Parents Can Do[9]

For parents, the following indicators are warning signs that your child might be getting bullied:

- physical signs – unexplained bruises, scratches, cuts or damage to clothes or belongings
- stress-caused illnesses – pains, headaches and stomach aches which seem unexplained
- fearful behaviour – fear of walking to school, taking different routes, asking to be driven
- a dropping-off in quality of schoolwork
- coming home hungry (perhaps lunch or lunch money is being stolen)
- asking for or stealing money (to pay the bully)

- having few friends
- rarely being invited to parties
- changes in behaviour – withdrawn, stammering, moody, irritable, upset, unhappy, tearful or distressed
- not eating
- attempting suicide or hinting at suicide
- anxiety – shown by bed-wetting, nail-biting, fearfulness, tics, not sleeping or crying out in sleep
- refusal to say what is wrong, and
- giving improbable excuses for any of the above.

Of course, there are other possible reasons for many of the above, and you should also get a doctor to check that those physical symptoms do not have another cause. A good doctor can also gently question your child to find out about bullying.

While the above may sound somewhat obvious, the fact is that boys often won't talk about bullying in the first instance because it seems weak to do so. Also, they may have been threatened with consequences if they tell, or they might fear it will make things worse to speak up.

If your child is being bullied, talk to the school, be calm, and take along written details of what has happened to your child. Expect that two or even three meetings may be necessary to give the school time to investigate and decide what to do. Don't 'give them a serve' and leave them to it. It will have to be a joint effort. Either you or a school counsellor can also work with your child to practise assertiveness, giving humorous replies to name-calling, telling bullies 'leave me alone, I don't like it', and acting and sounding determined. In primary school, a boy who knows how to make friends and avoid trouble, and who can speak up for himself, is generally ignored by bullies. Rigby and Slee recommend martial-arts training as a way to build physical confidence and assertiveness for children who are getting victimised a lot.

Avoid schools that are too big and impersonal. The limits to what can function as a caring community are about 400 pupils in a primary school and about 600 in a secondary school respectively. Anything larger will often become an inefficient education 'factory'.

Kids will join gangs for self-protection, and bullying will be a natural side effect of this.

Schools that are less competitively based, such as the Steiner and other alternative schools, generally have a more caring atmosphere in which children and teachers are closer and more involved, and bullying is uncommon. A very gentle child may benefit from a move to such a school.

Almost every child, boy or girl, will experience bullying and, if helped to acquire assertive skills, will overcome it. Most schools around the country are introducing the methods described here, but perhaps yours needs some encouragement. All of us – families, schools and society – need to learn to live without intimidation of each other.

4. Education with Energy

The learning environment of schools seems designed to educate senior citizens, not young people at their most energetic. Everyone is supposed to be quiet, nice and compliant. Excitement doesn't seem to belong in this kind of learning (though many wonderful teachers do manage to bring some fun and energy into their classes, and many children catch this spirit and run with it).

The passivity required by school contradicts everything we know about kids, especially adolescents. Adolescence is the age of passion. Boys (and girls) crave an engaged and intense learning experience, with men and women who challenge them and get to know them personally – and, from this specific knowledge of their needs, who work with them to shape and extend their intellect, spirit and skills. If kids aren't waking up in the morning saying, 'Wow! School today!', then something is not right.

Some kids are more passionate than others. Their specific passions and talents (not just their testosterone levels) make certain kids itch to do something of significance, something real and socially useful, or something really creative. If this vitality is not engaged with, it turns into misbehaviour and troublemaking.

The passion in the child has to be matched with an equal invest-ment from the parents, teachers or other mentors. The old initi-ators weren't casual or laid back – they took boys into the desert and taught them one-to-one about life-and-death concerns. Their graduation ceremonies were powerful and significant events for the young men. In other cultures, boys would dance non-stop all night, or walk 300 kilometres to fetch material for their initiation. These societies understood something about the energies of adolescence.

5. The Principal Is the Key

A male principal or senior teacher is an important, symbolic figure in children's minds – something between a father-substitute and a god-substitute! Knowing this, he must make it his business to know the kids, especially the high-risk boys and girls, long before they get into trouble. Then, if there's a problem, the relationship is already established and it's easier to talk things through.

A principal is also the key to getting boys to take on leadership roles, which these days they commonly reject. School principal Peter Ireland wrote in *Boys in Schools*[10] about a strategy he implemented at MacKillop Senior College, in regional New South Wales. Peter began regular schoolyard meetings with selected boys to build up their sense of belonging and participation in the life of the school. The meetings focused on understanding the boys' view of school, the impediments to their involvement, and how to solve these. The boys who participated in these meetings became significantly more involved in both their own studies and the community life of the school. They just needed encouragement.

6. Helping Boys with Their Vulnerable Areas

Language and expression are two specific weak areas for boys. As we've explained earlier, boys' brains are wired in a way that makes it harder for them to take feelings and impressions from the right side of their brain and put these into words into the left side.[11] They need extra help to master written language, to express themselves verbally and to learn to enjoy reading. Special programmes for boys in English, reading and drama are urgently needed from kindergarten upwards. In 'The Cotswold Experiment' (see page 160) we can see how one school tackled this problem, with spectacular results.

STORIES FROM THE HEART

THE COTSWOLD EXPERIMENT

Two big debates keep rearing their heads in the world of education, even making it onto the front pages of the newspapers.

The first is about single-sex schools versus co-education. Are boys and girls better off being separated? Boys not only do poorly at school, but their behaviour often prevents girls and quieter boys from learning. Parents of girls solve the problem by enrolling their daughters in girls-only schools. But where can the boys run to?

The second debate is about the decline in boys' attainment and participation at school, which has been noted in most industrial countries. Boys are doing poorly in relation to girls, especially in subjects like English, Art, the humanities and languages.

This problem tested the mind of Marion Cox, Head of English at The Cotswold School, a co-educational secondary school in the countryside in England. Marion decided to conduct an experiment. She assigned boys and girls in the fourth year of secondary school to gender-

segregated English classes, where they remained for two years. (In all other subjects, they still studied together in the conventional way.)

As the new, single-sex classes got under way, teachers adjusted the curriculum (e.g., the choice of books and poems) to make it more interesting for the boys or girls in their class. They were no longer restricted by trying to strike a middle path between the interests of boys and girls. The classes started to take on distinctly boy and girl flavours.

Class sizes were kept to about twenty-one per class – smaller than the average before the study. In addition, some intensive writing and reading support (encouragement and supervision to read in class time) was introduced for the boys.

THE RESULTS?

The results were impressive. According to national statistics for the United Kingdom, only 9 per cent of fourteen-year-old boys nationwide achieve grades in the range of A to C for English.[12] (English is not a subject that boys either like or do well in!) In the Cotswold School, following two years of separate classes, 34 per cent of boys scored in the A to C range in their final exams. The school had increased the number of boys in the high-scoring range by almost 400 per cent!

And the girls did better, too! An impressive 75 per cent of girls scored in the A to C range compared with 46 per cent the previous year. (Note that the girls' results were still dramatically higher than the boys!)

The gender separation effects caused considerable excitement around the UK. Marion Cox told *The Times* newspaper that the benefits went far beyond just English scores. 'Behaviour, concentration and reading levels all improved significantly. I believe if we can catch them even younger than fourteen, before they give up books for television and the computer, and the anti-heroic role models are entrenched, we would have even better chances of success.'

A GOOD ALTERNATIVE TO SINGLE-SEX SCHOOLS

When I spoke to Marion Cox by phone, she explained that boys at the school found they could relax and express themselves more without girls present, and girls reported the same. She felt that separation 'just for English' was a good alternative to the more extreme solution of single-sex schools. Marion noted that, 'The most frequent observation from visitors to our classes was that the atmosphere was more calm and settled. Boys were learning to enjoy reading – often for the first time.'

The Cotswold experiment did two things:

1. It acknowledged that boys generally have a slower acquisition of language skills, and helped them with this.
2. It gave boys a safe environment where they wouldn't feel stupid in front of the girls, who were so much more articulate. The boys didn't have to 'play up' to cover up their inadequacies, and they began to take 'risks' by reading and writing poetry, acting in plays, and so on.

Segregating classes and the curriculum is not risk-free. There is always a danger of reintroducing stereotypes: boys study war; girls study love! A lot depends on the teacher's attitude. The Cotswold results are encouraging: when separated, the girls and boys seemed able to relax and drop the old roles. The boys became more expressive and open; the girls more assertive. It seems to be an approach where everybody wins.

STORIES FROM THE HEART

HOMEWORK HELL

Every time I talk to parents, someone asks about which school to choose for their son.

The questionnaire later in this chapter (called 'How to tell if a school is a good one for boys' on page 169) is a big help with this, but there is another factor.

Often the best-equipped and prestigious schools are also the unhappiest, because of one word – pressure. Pressure of a kind that actually destroys kids' love of learning. And this is nowhere more obvious than in the scourge of homework. Many psychologists and counsellors now believe homework, beyond some simple revision, does more harm than good. Let this letter, which a distressed, yet very articulate mother sent to me, explain why.

Dear Steve,

My son's school is potentially a wonderful school. It has a wealth of facilities, labs, art rooms, auditoriums, sports fields, and so on. It has some exceptional teachers. Boys at the school are winning sporting events, gaining high marks, achieving excellence in music, art and drama.

However, there is something insidious happening at the school, which causes many boys great distress and turns others away from academic pursuits for life. A misdirected emphasis, an imbalance. I refer of course to the academic pressure, and one manifestation – homework.

The school resolutely demands that boys from the age of eight years onwards complete an extremely heavy homework load every night, regardless of everything else that is happening in the boy's (and his family's) life. It's so depressing for a parent to hear a Prep boy say he has 'heaps' of homework, and see him dejected and tired instead of happy to face an evening at home. It is devastating to see a fourteen-year-old boy (who has grown an inch in the last ten weeks) trudge home and tearfully say he just can't do any homework tonight. He falls asleep in his clothes, knowing he will have drills and detentions the following day. Are the expectations productive? Would one hour's homework a night in Year 10 give the same HSC result as three hours?

Parents end up supervising – and harassing – boys who work before dinner and then into the night. Surely it is more logical to set a small amount of homework and teach boys to work on their own; self-motivated work must be more valuable than work completed in anger and frustration. But will the boy who has tried against all the odds to achieve the three hours of compulsory homework a night give up, lose himself in despair, and vow to never pursue a career with university requirements? Worst of all, will he abhor intellectual inquiry ever after?

There are other negative effects that homework has, not only on the boy but on his home too. A boy gets up at 6.30 a.m. to leave home by 7.30 a.m. for school, and three out of four afternoons gets home at 6.00 p.m. or 6.30 p.m. He has to have time for dinner. Then it is homework. Shouldn't a boy be expected to take some responsibility for the smooth running of the household in which he lives? But when? It is the mothers who pick up the pieces when the boy is in despair of ever achieving the expectations set. The school is setting a blueprint for many boys – that they will never achieve reward for their effort – and is expecting families to wait on boys, with clothes, meals and transport, all to support the superhuman study effort. This conditions boys to expect the same from their spouses – which in the twenty-first century is not going to happen.

When do the boys get to play? Boys should have time to play the way they choose, to pursue their passions, relax and chat outside school.

Surely a school should build up the confidence of young boys, give them achievable goals and give them opportunity and encouragement to have fun. Fun can only be had if the boy is relaxed and comfortable in his environment.

It would be to the school's credit if it could take a lead and stand above the destructive values that society has adopted. Take a stand by saying that music is for pleasure and sport is for fun – and that is what this school will teach its boys, so that as adults they will still be playing their musical instruments, still be playing their chosen sports, still debating, still acting in plays, because school made it fun and something they want to take into their adult lives.

Has my son's school got the guts to take a stand? I don't think so.

And my two bob's worth? I think homework doesn't fit in with the modern world. It's not proven to be of any value until the later years of high school, and even then an hour is plenty. Families need more time now to connect, kids need more exercise and peace. Stress is an epidemic. It's time for homework to go.

Helping Boys Helps Girls Too

Thinking about boys' needs sometimes worries those who have worked hard to raise girls' attainment. They fear that girls might be 'pushed back into their box'. My experience is that nothing is going to stop girls now, though of course we must still be active and organised in helping them, as new assaults on girldom come from the media and from the neglect of parents to really help and support them.

But one of the greatest needs girls have is for boys to change. In wanting to create a good learning environment, and a safe world, girls' and boys' needs are deeply intertwined.

The boys-versus-girls debate is quite unnecessary. What the Cotswold experiment shows is that everyone can benefit if we tailor programmes to each 'special needs' group in the school. Boys, girls, low-income groups, ethnic groups, and so on all present different challenges. Everyone is human, everyone is special, and everyone deserves to be treated according to their individual needs. This is the way forward for schooling.

7. Role-modelling Is How Humans Learn

The role-model concept cannot be emphasised enough – it keeps cropping up with every teacher we talk to. Role-modelling is wired-in as an evolutionary trait in humans. We are a species that has few instincts, and must learn complex skills to survive. By watching a person we admire in action, our brain takes in a cluster of skills, attitudes and values. We don't need our role models to be great heroes – in some ways it's preferable to simply have people who are accessible and whom we like. An adolescent is a role-seeking missile, and he or she will lock-on to a range of targets before they have 'downloaded' enough material to shape their own identity.

A role model has to be seen by the teenager as 'someone like me' or 'someone I could be like'. Girls need role models at least

ROLE-SEEKING MISSILE

as much as boys, but girls get far more role models in school, and those women teachers often seem to share more of themselves. Consequently, girls drink in far more data on how to be a woman than boys do on how to be a man.

Role models can be surprising and diverse. They must also challenge and stretch youngsters' ideas. In the fairly impoverished outer-suburban high school I attended in the 1960s, I can remember some men who were positive gems:

- A maths teacher, who was also our home-group teacher, visited every child's parents at home (causing a spate of renovation and new furniture purchases through the year). The purpose of the visits was to persuade parents to let us stay at school for longer (at a time when finishing Year 12 was seen as a pretty ambitious thing to do). Although quite a slave driver in the classroom, this man also took us on the first long school excursion ever – a wonderful experience. He later became a well-known professor of education.
- An elderly man, an old soldier who cycled to work, taught us to love poetry. He inflicted Shakespeare on us even though it wasn't on the curriculum, but also took us bushwalking, taught yoga, and gave up many weekends to take us on hikes and camping trips.
- A radical communist English teacher, who warned us about the escalating Vietnam War, told us about social advances in Russia, and got us to read *To Kill a Mockingbird* and *Shane*.
- An electronics whiz spent lunchtimes with kids who wanted to make and mend radios.

Along with cheerful sports teachers and plenty of great women teachers, school really did broaden our horizons on what being male could be about.

STORIES FROM THE HEART

A HIGH SCHOOL DOING A GREAT JOB WITH BOYS

Staff at Ashfield Boys High School, in Sydney's inner west, wanted to make learning more personal, believing that the closer the relationship between the teacher and the student, the more effective the learning would be.

'We were trying to analyse what was wrong. The boys were not as engaged with learning and were not as successful as they should be,' Ashfield principal Ann King told Jane Figgis in the *Sydney Morning Herald*.[13] So Ashfield restructured its Year 7 and 8 classes in a dramatic way. 'Instead of having ten to thirteen teachers, boys now have a team of five teachers, who not only teach but are responsible for discipline, welfare and parent liaison.'

Sessions have been extended from the usual 40 minutes to 80 or 100 minutes, after it was realised students were having small parcels of learning that were not connected.

'We have found it works tremendously well,' Ms King says. 'On many measures we are seeing that they are more actively and success-fully engaged in their learning. The real value, however, of teaching teams and students who stay together as a group through the school day, and year, is the potential for the students and their teachers to develop much more solid and collaborative relationships.'

Relationships are the key to middle schooling (Years 7, 8 and 9). 'Students and teachers have to learn to listen to each other, to trust each other, to like each other. They need to be able to challenge each other, but that can only happen when they feel at ease and secure in the relationship,' said Ms King.

(In my book *The New Manhood*[14] we detail other special programmes for boys in schools, including NITOR for disengaged boys, and The Rite Journey, which provides a one year rite of passage built in to Year 9. Both of these and similar programmes transform the lives of thousands of boys in schools worldwide.)

PRACTICAL HELP

HOW TO TELL IF A SCHOOL IS A GOOD ONE FOR BOYS[15]

How do you know if a school is going to be good for your son? Apart from the obvious – happy, courteous and cheerful kids in the school grounds and happy, courteous and cheerful staff in the building – there are some more questions to ask.

You might not want to use all of these, but they are a good guide. And for a school evaluating itself, they are vital.

- It knows how it is doing with boys, and can tell you. The school keeps track of how individual boys, and boys as a whole, are doing on a range of criteria, including engagement in school activities and school life, academic effort, progress and results, behaviour and relationships, sporting and social life, and leadership.

Key question: What statistics does the school publish about boys' progress?

- It has policies and practices based on a positive approach to maleness. The school knows what it values in boys and men, based on asking parents, teachers, girls and boys themselves, and it celebrates and honours this positive view of what boys can be.

Key question: Does the school have a mission statement about which qualities it likes, wants and values in boys?

- It uses teaching and assessment styles that appeal to boys' strengths. This means recognising the likely maturational, physical and social differences between boys and girls, and having positive approaches to these – e.g. possible late starting for boys, physical and activity-based teaching and assessment methods in all grades and all subjects, and catering for kinaesthetic, visual and musical intelligence as well as linguistic and logical intelligence.

Key question: How does the school accommodate the specific developmental, physical, social and learning needs of boys in its teaching and assessment?

- It has behaviour policies and procedures that help boys gain a positive identity, and a positive relationship with others. This means that discipline or behaviour procedures are based on agreed values, with the aim of having fair, equitable and fun relationships between everyone in the school. Male and female staff should be good models of this type of relationship.

Key question: Do teachers shout at children at this school?

- It has school structures that are likely to suit boys. This means having a flexible approach to timetabling, which can allow for:
  - single-sex classes for some subjects at certain ages (e.g. Year 3 and the middle-school years)
  - school-to-work programmes
  - longer class periods in the morning
  - fewer changes of teacher, and
  - two-year blocks with the same teacher.

Key question: How does the timetable allow for boys' special need for more settled (in terms of teachers) and sometimes separate learning?

- It ensures that boys have access to a range of male mentors and role models. This means recognising that male staff and volunteers have a special role in relation to boys. It also requires tackling the question of what qualities the school seeks in its male staff (apart from just being male).

Key question: What personality criteria are used to select male staff at this school?

- It is democratic. This means that for all students, including boys, there should be real participation in deciding how the school is run – not just in the style of uniform, but in the real issues of classroom learning and what the school offers.

Key question: How are boys involved in decision-making here?

- It offers many different ways to gain recognition. Not all boys are good at maths or football. There needs to be ways in which all boys can gain recognition. Highly competitive regimes, with prizes for only the top few, do not suit boys.

Key question: How do shy, overweight, arty or simply average boys achieve recognition at this school?

- It involves fathers and father figures from the community. In most schools, the ratio of female to male volunteers is about 6:1. It is a myth that dads are too busy, or don't care, or aren't good at school activities. But they will not get involved without some real creative effort from the school.

Key question: What is your strategy for getting dads and other community men involved?

- It is continually active in learning how to do better with boys. Men and women teachers can learn from each other about what works and why. Because new issues about boys' education are coming to light, there should be ongoing in-service training, research and evaluation regarding effective education for boys.

Key question: Do you have ongoing staff development and research into what works best for boys within the school?

WHAT ARE 'LEARNING DIFFICULTIES'?

Almost everyone has some brain damage. Small amounts of damage may take place at birth, or are caused by blows to the head, genetic impairment, mercury or lead in the environment, or by parents smoking or drinking during pregnancy. Boys are more prone to brain damage, though the reasons for this are not well understood.

Minor brain damage isn't a problem, unless your child has some trouble with learning. In the past, many learning problems passed unnoticed because a high level of literacy was less important. Today they can be a real disadvantage – but luckily, a lot can be done to help.

There are four main types of learning difficulty, and these relate to the way information is processed. For a child to learn, information has to do four things: it has to go into his brain through his sensory nerves, get organised to make sense, be kept there in the memory, and then be brought out again when needed. Let's take a look at these steps.

1. *Input* This might mean hearing a teacher properly, being able to understand what is shown in a book, or following instructions. Sometimes a parent can be infuriated that a child just isn't 'getting it' – yet it mightn't be the child's fault. Sometimes children literally don't hear or see what we hear or see. Listen to this boy describing his sensory problems: 'I used to hate small shops because my eyesight used to make them look smaller than they actually were. Another trick which my ears played was to change the volume of sounds around me. Sometimes when other kids spoke to me I could scarcely hear them, and sometimes they sounded like bullets. I thought I was going to go deaf.' (Darren, aged twelve)[16]

2. *Organisation* This involves the child adding an instruction (i.e. to organise) to the others he already has, summing up the input content for himself – so he does not, for instance, see the number 231, but store it as 213).

3. *Memory* Everyone knows about this one! When the child goes to get it out again, it's still there! There are both short-term and long-term memory abilities – and sometimes one and not the other is impaired.

4. *Output* Can the child make sense as he speaks, writes or draws? The knowledge is in there – can he get it out?

"In a sense Jane Eyre epitomised a generational shift."

YUP

OUTPUT DIFFICULTY

Clearly, it's wise to get professional help if you suspect your child is having trouble. Many learning difficulties can be overcome, or at least minimised. The earlier you act, the easier this will be.

OCCUPATIONAL THERAPY

Here is an instance of a boy overcoming an output problem – handwriting.

David, aged eight, had a lot of trouble with handwriting. Poor handwriting isn't unusual for boys at this age, but David's parents were worried because he hadn't improved at all for two years. They knew David was a bright child but feared that, because of his poor written work, teachers might think he was dumb.

The normal way to improve handwriting is through lots of practice – practising big swirls and shapes, getting smaller, learning individual letters, gradually building up the skills of easy writing. But David's parents spoke to someone who suggested they try something else as well – occupational therapy.

Kerry Anne Brown, an occupational therapist experienced in children's learning difficulties, agreed to see David for an evaluation. Kerry Anne discovered that David was poorly coordinated in his whole upper body, not just in his hands. In fact it was hard for him to write well because he did not sit well or hold his arms in a strong, firm way.

David began doing exercises (for balance, like spinning and trampolining) to strengthen his back muscles and build up the coordination of his back, shoulders and arms. This required a six-month programme of about half an hour a day. Luckily, these kinds of exercises were quite good fun, and his dad and mum enjoyed the exercise time with him. Sometimes the harder parts made David grumpy, but overcoming frustration is part of any new learning. His parents cajoled and humoured him, and kept him going. After about six months, the programme was getting good results, and they were able to stop.

Three years later, David still has to 'make himself' write well – relax his body, and really pay attention. But his writing is now good for a boy his age. Although he would rather use a computer to write, he enjoys creative writing, and was recently the highest ranking student in his primary school.

Parents Make It Happen

Learning difficulties require two things – time and resources – and these have to be fought for. Kids whose parents care about them and are willing to spend time with them will always fare better. It takes determination – tracking down specialist help, refusing to be ignored or fobbed off, and pushing the school system to get special help. Be sure to talk to other parents, and be proactive until something happens that works for your child.

Resources include special programmes or equipment, specialist teachers and classes, and things you can do at home. Meeting other parents whose children have the same problem as your child can be a huge help – it's great to get information and emotional support from people who really understand.

A note of caution: occasionally you may encounter schools that do not want to know about kids with learning difficulties. They are more interested in the elite achievers, who keep up the school's academic average. A child with a learning difficulty might actually be pressured to leave, or just not be helped. Caring schools will always do their best, and you wouldn't want your child to attend a school that did not care for all its kids, anyway.

IN A NUTSHELL

Schools can be good places for boys if they do the following:

- Allow boys to start more formal schooling one year later than girls, when their fine-motor skills are ready for pencil-and-paper work (girls' skills develop more quickly).
- Vigorously recruit males (both young and mature in age) into teaching, and also involve more of the right kind of men from the community to provide one-to-one coaching and support.
- Re-design schooling to be more physical, energetic, concrete and challenging.
- Target boys' weak areas (literacy especially) with boy-specific intensive language programmes, right from Grade 1 (and have separate English classes in mid-high school).
- Build good personal relationships with boys, through smaller groupings and fewer teacher changes in high school, so as to meet boys' needs for fathering and mentoring.
- Be alert to the fact that problem behaviour can be a sign of learning difficulties, and investigate this as soon as possible.

Chapter 9

Boys and Sport

For most boys, sport is a huge part of life. It can do them a lot of good. It can give them a sense of belonging, develop character, and boost self-esteem and good health. Most dads and many mums reading this will remember sport as a great part of their childhood. It provides fun, friendship and fitness, a pretty unbeatable package. But it can also do a lot of harm: it can cripple boys in body, warp them in mind, teach them bad values and lead to a crushing sense of failure.

All through our history, human beings have played sport. Even in the Dark Ages, people played early forms of football. Almost all cultures had running races. The Romans had gladiators and the Greeks had the Olympics. And while not solely a male preserve, sport has appealed to boys especially – perhaps as an outlet for their explosive energies and a chance to excel at something that doesn't require talking or neatness!

Sport means respect – in most industrial nations today, it is virtually a sacred activity. No religion comes close in its passion, the sheer number of its adherents or its power to inspire. So, for every parent of boys, dealing with sport is a major interest and challenge.

Christmas Cricket

Every Christmas, our extended family gathers together from far and wide in Tasmania. We oldies watch with delight as the youngsters are instantly at ease again, as if the intervening year since last Christmas simply hadn't happened.

We eat Poppy and Nana's cooking, then settle down to a game of cricket in the paddock out the back. I've watched this for twenty years now, since the children could barely hold on to a bat. It's a very child-oriented game, and no one keeps score.

What is most amazing in these once-a-year games is the way that the men, normally quiet guys on the whole, seem to come out of themselves on the cricket pitch. A little boy attempts to bat; the men praise and encourage him, visibly leaning closer as if to will him to success. An eight-year-old struggles with overarm bowling, and sends the ball wildly off course; old men call out, 'Good one!' and, 'That's better!' Small hints are whispered. Somebody rushes in to correct a grip. A kid gets out for a duck and is allowed to stay in so he can have a hit.

It's not all peace and light. Two of the ten-year-old boys are at the stage of being obsessed with rules. There is a dispute; a boy yells abuse. His father takes him off to the side for a quiet talking-to. The gist of it is, 'Feelings are important here. It's only a game' – a hard thing for a ten-year-old to digest. Sport is a lot about character-building.

Play goes on. I think of this tradition of caring for the young that goes back to the very roots of human history. Sport can be an unbeatable medium for caring, learning and bringing the generations together.

The Positives of Sport

Sport can be a beautiful part of life. If adults understand sport, enjoy it with their kids, guide their kids into the right attitudes, and remember what sport is for, then all will be well.

Helping Men and Boys Get Close

Sport offers a boy a chance to get closer to his father, and to other boys and men, through a common interest they might otherwise lack. Complete strangers can discuss it – including fathers and sons!

Many men will tell you, 'If my old man and I couldn't talk about sport, we'd have nothing to talk about at all.'

Sport is a way of joining the community. Immigrant children arriving at school are immediately asked which football team they support! And refugee boys and men often distinguish themselves and find a welcome through sporting prowess.

A Safe Place to Show Affection

A friend of mine was once persuaded to join a men's indoor cricket team. He wasn't keen. To use his own words, he expected to be 'bored stupid by macho rubbish'. But he was amazed to find it was nothing like that. The men were incredibly affectionate towards each other. There was real praise for effort, an exchange of hints and skills, warmth and (through good-natured teasing) much affirmation of the younger men's energy and skill, and the older men's experience and perspective. And in the after-game sessions, real concerns and life challenges were discussed. The thing that struck my friend was that he knew some of these men in their families and in the business world, and they were nothing like this anywhere else. Somehow the structure and rituals of the team allowed each man to be a fuller, happier self. My friend enjoyed the experience immensely.

Lessons for Life

Because sport is the main place where men and boys interact, it is often where boys can work through in a practical way their values for life. From a tender age, when they can barely hold a bat or ball, little boys begin to learn how to:

• be a good loser (and not cry or punch someone or run away if you lose)

- be a good winner (be modest and not get too 'up yourself', and so avoid ill feeling)
- be part of a team (to play cooperatively, recognise your limitations, and support others' efforts)
- give it your best effort (training even when you are tired, and keeping on trying your hardest)
- work for a long-term goal or objective (and making sacrifices to achieve it), and
- see that almost everything you do in life improves with practice.

Parents will go to endless trouble so that their kids can play sport. The benefits are clear – fun, fitness and fresh air, character-building, friendship, and a sense of achievement and belonging. And the kids get a lot out of it, too!

The Negatives

On the other side of the coin, sport is changing, and not always for the better. There are hazards to body and mind, and parents have to steer a little more carefully than a generation ago. Let's explore why.

STORIES FROM THE HEART

THE TIGER ELEVEN

It was 2002, and Australia was deeply divided about refugees from the Middle East. Our government had imprisoned over 4,000 asylum seekers – mostly families, including mothers and tiny babies – in detention camps.

A woman farmer from outback Queensland, Camilla Cowley, decided she had to do something to break down the prejudices which made this cruelty possible. She formed the Tiger Eleven Soccer Team, made up of Hazara (Afghan) teenage boys who had fled the Taliban (who would have killed them or forced them to be soldiers) and finally been released from detention after community pressure. The team toured the country, boarding in homes, playing local school teams and being interviewed in local papers. I spoke to one boy – he had not heard from his family for two years and feared they were dead. Australian kids were often afraid of playing soccer against 'terrorists' – did they carry knives in their soccer shorts? But the effect of meeting these gentle, shy and brave kids of fourteen and fifteen years of age, playing sport against them, laughing and chatting to them afterwards, transformed thousands of kids and their communities. Sport had provided a medium for trust.

Toxic Role Models and the 'Jock' Culture

Sport and sporting heroes are an obsession for our whole society. Imagine if someone suggested that we devote the last ten minutes of the evening news to woodwork or stamp collecting! Sports stars set fashion trends, command huge incomes, and carry the hope of national pride. Sportspeople are recognised, while great musicians, artists and writers of parenting books are barely noticed.

We parents want to use the power of sport to make our kids better people. But it can just as easily work the other way: especially in male sport, impressionable children learn all kinds of unwholesome messages from men who never really grew up. (When Donald Trump boasted of molesting women, his defenders said it was just 'locker-room talk'. Like, that's what athletes do all the time.)

Where are you most likely to see real-life demonstrations of violence, egotism, bad temper, sexual crudity, alcohol abuse, racism and homophobia? At any big sports game! A boy might learn to be courageous and strong by playing rugby or football, but he might also learn to binge-drink, use drugs and mistreat women.

Sports' leaders are like elders of the tribe. They set the tone. If sport doesn't better equip our youngsters for real life, then we are better off going fishing.

The Talent Trap

Success can be a much bigger problem than failure. Few boys today get adequate male attention. If a boy shows promise in football, baseball, cricket or tennis, then adults suddenly begin to take an interest in him. His father or coach showers him with praise. His name and photo are in the local paper, strangers congratulate him in the street. The men are getting a vehicle for their own frustrated dreams; the boy is getting the approval he craves. Being a sports hero gives a boy an artificial sense of his own importance. His access to adoring girls and even adult 'sucking up' will set him up for an inevitable collision with reality.

But what if the boy injures himself? What if he reaches his natural limitations? What if he resorts to performance-enhancing drugs to keep up with expectations? The approval falls away, the older men show their disappointment. Community praise turns to rejection. Thousands of young lives have been harmed in this way. The more talented a child is, the more important it is that parents guard against 'sports abuse' – not letting the normal tasks of adolescence be disrupted by an adult agenda.[1]

STORIES FROM THE HEART

THE COACH FROM HELL!

Fourteen-year-old Leith was keen on rugby. Because his school didn't field a team for his age group, his dad took him to a local club that had an under-15s team. This team had made it to the grand final three years in a row, but never quite clinched that final game.

To overcome this, a special coach was hired – an ex-footballer, large and aggressive – to train the forwards. Leith's father, Jeff, watched from the sidelines as the new coach spoke to the boys one night close to the big match. He was shocked to hear his instructions. 'As soon as you have your first run-in with the other team's players, I want you to hit them hard in the face.'

One of the boys wasn't sure if he'd heard right. 'Is that, uh, if they hit you, do you mean?' he stammered.

'No, you bloody idiot,' (the coach talked like this all the time) 'you punch them before they get the chance. Understand?'

Jeff felt himself shaking with anger. He had to think this over. This was not his idea of what the sport was about. That night he phoned a friend who also coached rugby. He confirmed that punching was against the rules and could lead to a suspension – and was just plain wrong!

Jeff realised he had to have it out with the coach. He confronted him – not without trepidation, as the coach was a huge man. The coach dismissed him laughingly: 'Huh, those wimps, they wouldn't do it anyway! I'm just trying to give them some steel, the little pansies. They wouldn't do it!'

Jeff decided this wasn't any place for a boy to be learning the rules of life. Father and son talked it over, and Leith was happy to quit the team. Next year he played at his school, in a team that was coached by a better kind of man.

'Looking back,' Jeff told me later, 'I'd known all along that the team had no spirit – the coaches constantly put the boys down, there was no group feeling, no praise, no socialising or enjoyment. And despite making it to three grand finals, they were always made to feel like failures.'

Leith was a whole lot happier, and his dad was pleased to have recognised the problem and found a better alternative.

What About Injuries?

Sport is healthy, isn't it? Not always. Men's health researcher Richard Fletcher found that for some sports it was healthier to stay at home and watch television![2] Many top athletes and sportsmen have painful and crippling injuries by the time they are thirty. These range from head injuries through to countless damaged joints and tendons. Sporting sprains and pains often lead to painful arthritis in midlife. It's becoming clear that certain sports are no longer a good risk for kids.

In Australia, over 10,000 children a year are seen in hospital accident and emergency departments as a result of sporting injuries.[3]
About 2,000 of these injuries could be classed as serious, involving
long-term treatment or hospitalisation. Body-contact sports cause
the highest number of injuries, with rugby league/rugby union,
soccer (football), basketball, cricket and netball topping the list in
that order.

Injuries sustained by school children playing sport include
sprains, strained muscles, bruising and breaks. There have been a
number of deaths of boys playing rugby in recent years, as well as
a worrying number of head injuries and spinal injuries. And sports
injuries increase with age: on average, between the ages of twelve
and sixteen, the injury rate increases sevenfold. The real problem
is competition. Being over-competitive leads to risk-taking, aggression, and going beyond sensible physical limits. Adults are to blame
for this. Children by and large prefer to have fun; they are not fanat-
ical unless we make them so.

This shouldn't be taken to mean keeping your boys away from
sport. The need to test oneself in physical ways, to experience
moderate levels of competition – for the fun of it – and the sheer
benefits of spending lots of time being active and in the open air
means that sport is always going to be a winner for boys' health and
development. We just have to choose the sport carefully, be involved
in seeing that it's well run, and the sport is for the kids, not the other
way around.

Most dangerous sports – Rugby League; Rugby Union

Second-most dangerous sports – Australian Rules Football;
Boxing; Grass Skiing; Ice Hockey; Parachuting; Skateboarding

Third-most dangerous sports – Cycling; Hockey

Safer sports – Basketball; Cricket; Gymnastics; Netball;
Soccer (Football); Squash; Touch Football

PRACTICAL HELP

ROLE-MODELLING

The nature of youngsters is to take in their role models and swallow them whole. Luckily, as we mature as a society, we find there are more diverse ways to be a man. A boy might admire and find tuition from a musician, an artist, a craftsman, a movie-maker, a fly fisherman or a dancer, as much as from a sportsman. We must try and make it possible for every boy to find his true path – this means casting a wide net of possibilities. Perhaps, one day soon, we will have so many good men in the lives of children that kids will be able to develop a widely based, rich and really life-inspiring identity. 'That man is like me, and I can be like that man' will be true for every boy.

IN A NUTSHELL

Sport can have huge benefits for children. It gives exercise, fun, challenges and a sense of achievement. It especially provides a shared interest between fathers and sons, and between boys and men generally.

- Sport is often a great way of building character, learning about life and developing masculinity.
- Unfortunately, sport is changing for the worse. The culture of some sports encourages negative traits like aggression, egotism, sexual crudity and binge-drinking. And 'winning at all costs' is replacing sportsmanship and the pleasure of playing the game for its own sake.
- When competition and winning are made so important, it is dangerous to be talented, because your life can become unbalanced. Playing sport too competitively often leads to lifelong injuries.
- Emphasising competition excludes many kids who are not so talented.
- Sport must be participatory, safe, non-elitist, and fun for everyone. Boys need sport. We must not let it be spoiled by commercial forces or toxic leadership.

Chapter 10

A Community Challenge

Eventually, the spirit of a boy grows too great for just a family to contain, and his horizons are wider than a family can provide for. By mid-teens, a boy wants to leap into his future – but there must be a place for him to leap to, and strong arms to steady him. This means building community links in order to help boys take the last big step to adulthood.

If we parents have 'community' around us, then we know that other adults, singly or as an organised group, can support our teenagers into a sense of worth and belonging. Without community – networks of committed adults consciously caring for each other's children – adolescence can actually fail as a stage.

The transition into adulthood takes a concerted effort. But how is this done? What are the methods and what is the timetable? What are the key elements? Some are practical: a listening ear, the teaching of skills, the expansion into new horizons of thinking and action, the giving of cautions, and protection from danger. Some are more 'magical' and spiritual.

To illustrate, and to give a fitting ending to this book, I have chosen three stories. Each is a story about community action turning boys into men. Each story is very different – a football match, a school on the poor side of town, and an island sojourn. I hope you enjoy them.

STORIES FROM THE HEART

LOSING, WINNING AND GRACE

The annual match between Sydney's two proudest Catholic private schools, St Joseph's College and Riverview, has always taken epic proportions in the minds of those who follow rugby union.

St Joseph's record against all schools is somewhat awesome. It was the kind of record that gave mystical impossibility to the idea of wresting it from them!

In 1996, however, it was different. Riverview knew they had a great team, capable of achieving the impossible. So on this day, under a clear blue sky, there was a special sense of history. As the game progressed, it became evident to the 15,000 or so parents and Old Boys who gathered to watch that the unthinkable was going to happen – St Joseph's were going to lose the day. Despite valiant attempts by the St Joseph's boys in the second half, clawing their way back on the scoreboard, the Riverview team held the lead. Soon the final siren signalled an end to St Joseph's' long reign.

The match was over – the victors punched the air and whooped about. Then something powerful and special began to take place. The losing team formed a ring on the oval, linked arms, and stood as if in prayer – absorbing not so much the loss as something more, perhaps the sense of shared effort, the sheer poignancy of the moment. Then the real magic began. Like an answer from around the stadium, men who had gone to that school, and fathers of the boys, walked towards the circle and wrapped their arms around the ring of boys. Several hundred men ended up in a silent, powerful ring of masculine grace.

People pouring from the stands froze in place and just watched. Losing or winning lost all meaning at the sight of this. It was the sense of union through effort, of giving yourself to something larger – as ancient as the mammoth hunt, the defence of the city, or the thousand other ways men have stood together for *good* reasons. And it was the honouring and welcoming of youth into its glory.

No one who was in that circle will forget it. Each became more of a man because of that day.

Rites of Passage

Two excellent programmes are now being used across Australia to help boys journey into manhood. Pathways to Manhood (www.pathwaysfoundation.com.au), is a camping programme which offers fathers an intensive sharing experience of helping their sons to become good men.

The Rite Journey (www.theritejourney.com) is an exciting new school-based programme that extends across the whole of Year 9. It helps boys think about manhood, become protective and self-aware, manage anger, and much more, in a moving and memorable way. The Rite Journey was developed in Lutheran schools and can be introduced through a training package to interested teachers.

STORIES FROM THE HEART

MEN AT WORK

A large company in New Zealand was wanting to do something for its local community – nothing altruistic about this, just good business sense. The usual thing might be to endow a youth centre or build a park. They were persuaded by some wise souls to adopt a local school in the run-down neighbourhood where their plant was situated – and to contribute not money, but time.

Every employee was given the opportunity to go to the school and offer one-to-one coaching to a child who needed help with maths, reading or motor skills. They could do this for two hours a week in work time. The school coordinated the programme, the company donated the manpower and womanpower.

The result was that at-risk children got two visits a week in school time from their own long-term special adult. The effect of the programme was so significant that over two years the school's national testing scores improved markedly. And that was only one outcome – think of the self-esteem, the mentoring and the long-term outcomes in turning kids towards positive lifestyles.

What would happen if we took the 'do-gooder' energies of our service clubs and corporations (and so on) and built human contact instead of, or as well as, chequebook approaches to making kids' lives a little richer? It's hard to know where such an involvement would stop. Getting to know kids in trouble changes your perspective; benefits flow both ways. Perhaps it would work in an organisation you belong to? This kind of thing *can* change the world.

STORIES FROM THE HEART

INITIATION

It's autumn on an island off Australia's beautiful coastline. Twelve men, with rucksacks and coats, and nine teenage boys ranging from fourteen to nineteen had jostled onto the ferry three days ago to cross to the island. Now they are awaiting its return to carry them home. Their mood is reflective and serene, like the glassy water around the sheltered landing place.

Seven of the boys are sons of the men; two are boys without fathers. Some of the men are married; a couple are separated. One is a single father.

Three days ago they had walked to a remote shack on the island, where they cooked lunch, explored, played and swam at a wild and windswept beach. At night, they carried coats and walked through the darkness to a place where a fire had been prepared beforehand, and sat down – the boys nervous and joking, wondering what was to happen.

Around the fire, each of the twelve men stood up and spoke about his own life. Some spoke with humour, some were faltering and emotional. After this, each father stood again and spoke on behalf of his own son. He spoke about the qualities of his son, his own special memories and how much he loved this boy. The boys without fathers received this praise equally from one of the men who was there to represent them – adding messages sent from a grandfather and a father in prison.

Fathers openly praising their sons! There was something so unique in this experience that many of the men and boys were wet-eyed in the half-light of the flames. Somehow these tears were soothing and sweet – the very opposite of grief or shame.

After the men finished, each boy then spoke for himself in reply (which they did with surprising eloquence) about his life, his values and hopes.

Several men read poems. A special story was told, which combined ritual elements from Aboriginal and Anglo-Celtic roots. They sang songs and had some supper and, in the early hours, walked back to the camp to sleep.

Later that weekend, the boys and men split into small groups, talking about the boys' plans for their lives and their goals for the coming year. These goals were announced ritually in a final meeting of the whole group. One boy wanted to go back to school and finish his HSC, another to get a job, another to stop depending on drugs, several to right wrongs they had committed, one to find a girlfriend, and another to 'make it work out with Mum'.

Adults offered support to each young man: one offered somewhere to study; another a meeting for coffee once a month to follow up. One man committed to drive a boy to Adelaide to make amends to a grandmother he had stolen money from and never owned up. The group agreed to meet one year later to reaffirm their care for the youngsters.

The stars were coming out in a vast banner above them as the boat made its way back across to the mainland to release them on their separate ways.

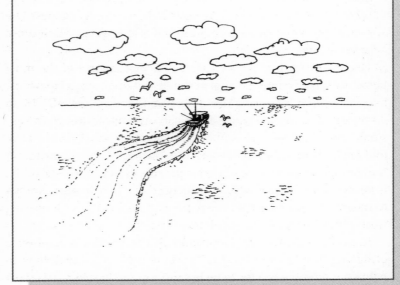

ADHD in Boys

ADHD is the name given to a syndrome or a cluster of problem behaviours – which has had a huge effect on the lives of boys, and some girls as well. This cluster usually includes distractibility, forgetfulness, poor impulse control, and hyperactivity – moving about all the time. It's not hard to spot.

Approximately 5 per cent of boys in the US, and somewhat less in various other countries, are given this diagnosis and treated with fairly significant amphetamine medication.[1] That such a disorder might occur – without explanation and without any known mechanism or physical cause – that requires one in twenty of the young male population to take strong medication to control, has shocked and concerned many commentators and practitioners. Is it our culture of rush and hurry from birth to the grave that prevents little children from learning to be calm and focused? Is it the way schools are, needing little boys to sit still? Is too much television preventing the skills of attention from developing? Is it stress at home, and parents not meeting children's needs early in life? Is it greedy drug companies wanting to hook everyone on their products? Is it something different in the brain? Is it passed on in a family's genes? The answer is probably a combination of all of these. And all of these offer some help.

Leading Canadian psychiatrist Gabor Mate is one of the most perceptive practitioner-writers in the field. Gabor was a Holocaust baby, born in a Nazi concentration camp, and he has ADHD. So do his three children. He uses medication himself, though in very small doses and only as needed. (Friends who know Gabor have told me he is very different when he is on and off the medication.) But, perhaps most hearteningly for parents of boys with ADHD, he is a hugely productive, valuable, focused and caring man, known to most Canadians for his newspaper columns and his pioneering work with Vancouver drug addicts.

In his book *Scattered*,[2] Gabor talks vividly about the experience of having ADHD from the inside. He doesn't give quick how-to help, though there is a lot to be learnt from reading him. His most important message is the belief, supported by very significant research, that ADHD is the result of stress, and is a unique response that only some individuals suffer. He believes:

- that what we label ADHD (and many similar so-called 'conditions') are on the normal spectrum of being human, and have potentialities and positives as well as costs. It comes to the fore especially in a modern world that both stresses us mentally and yet requires us to sit still and regulate ourselves in a machine-like way to the needs of society. It's hard having ADHD, and it requires a lot of love, understanding and help.
- that there are certainly inherited tendencies towards having ADHD, but these require stress or attachment difficulties in pregnancy, infancy or childhood to release their disturbing effects. Some babies are very high-need, and we have to work better to understand and care for them.
- that the parts of the brain that make us calm, able to focus, and feel safe and loved, actually develop during the second six months of life. Areas of the cortex are thinner in people with ADHD. Reducing stress on mothers and ensuring good attachment and empathy during the age of six months to one year may be crucial to preventing ADHD in vulnerable individuals.
- that ADHD management may involve drugs, but eventually depends on us becoming more self-regulating, learning to develop the skills of focus and calming.
- that nurturing kindness in the home and in the school is the key to managing this and many other developmental disorders, such as Asperger's, eating disorders and drug and alcohol addiction.

I would add to these: that ADHD is real. But it is also often over-diagnosed, and it's important to look at all possible causes – what might be stressing the child in his home, school, or other locations. All these possibilities have to be investigated before the label can be accurately applied, because many things in life make kids like this – abuse, family discord, trauma, grief, and so on.

Amphetamine medication is far from ideal. It becomes less effective over time, it has been associated with mental and also cardiac side effects, and is worryingly linked in some studies with chromosome abnormalities.[5]

On the plus side – it works. It can create a window in which a child can be helped and taught to learn, can self-manage his distractibility, and in which the family can learn routines and ways to help. But never depend just on medication alone to help your child, and work towards one day doing with less or none.

Along with Gabor Mate's book, some recommended books are listed in the Notes. Also, most libraries have a collection of good ADHD parenting books that they can recommend.

PRACTICAL HELP

BOYS AND BINGE DRINKING

Binge drinking is a problem, not for all teenagers but for a sector – perhaps the one in five who belong to a peer group that considers it normal behaviour to drink in order to be drunk.[3] And for these teens, away from proper adult care and exploited by venues and alcohol marketers, the danger is huge.

The award-winning youth support website reachout.com cautions young drinkers that binge drinking can be 'immediately and directly harmful to your health. It can expose you to injury or to unnecessary risks to yourself and others.' When kids get bashed, have bad sexual experiences, or are killed by vehicles, alcohol is nearly always involved.

There are lots of things that you can do to reduce your son's (or daughter's) chances of being harmed by alcohol. And luckily they are all just part of good parental care.

1. It used to be thought that being introduced to drinking at home, with early-mid teens being allowed a drink, was a preventative to misusing alcohol later. New research says the opposite. It is now

recommended that kids aren't given alcohol until they are eighteen – the same age they can legally buy it. This makes it special, links it with the responsibilities of adulthood, and sends a message that it is a privilege.[4]

2. Often kids' excessive drinking is tacitly approved, and in fact helped, by adults trying to be cool and gain favour with their offspring. Some parents supply alcohol for parties – this is a bad idea and a case of weak parenting.

3. Having teenage kids is actually a great reason to moderate your own drinking. If you see it as normal to have more than a couple of drinks at a certain time every day, and if alcohol is heavily consumed in the home, it's likely the kids will be problem drinkers, too.

4. Young people – i.e. under-eighteens – hanging about in large peer groups are a sign that adults and the community are not involved enough with their kids. Even eighteen-year-olds can fall victim to boredom and a lack of opportunities to mix with the opposite sex in safe settings, with older people available and looking out for them. Kids with interests – with active social lives built around doing things such as making music, playing sport, involved in outdoor activities, martial arts, youth groups or theatre and dancing, and so on – don't look to drinking as a recreation in itself.

5. Boys in particular, but also many girls, feel pressured to be sexually active, or at least to be paired up, when they are neither old enough nor emotionally ready. They feel acutely socially anxious, especially in large groups in noisy venues and out on the streets. (Clubs and pubs rarely have anywhere to even sit or talk quietly – they are designed to maximise drinking while on your feet.) Boys drink to get up the courage to approach girls, and vice versa. And while you may become more relaxed, you also lose the ability to converse, so this is not a very effective way to start a relationship. Kids may progress straight to (probably clumsy) sex because they are too anxious or drunk to talk.

Finally, as the generation of parents who have lived through a lot of changing values and confusion around alcohol, drugs and sex, we might feel confused ourselves about what is right and wrong. Our kids might actually want and need us to have clear values – to say no to going downtown on a Friday night to simply drift around; to want to know where they are and what they are doing. To set some boundaries. In other words, to care.

STORIES FROM THE HEART

HOW HAVING A SON HAS CHANGED ME

by Sarah MacDonald

Sarah MacDonald is an Australian writer, journalist and radio broadcaster who for a long time didn't understand males. Having a son changed everything. As she began to love him, it began to heal her too. A beautiful story to end the book.

I'm as much of a fan of martial arts as I am of major dental work. But this week, as I watched my little boy wrap a white belt around his skinny waist, join a line of his mates and learn to kick, my heart swelled with love. Having a son has changed so much about how I view the world. From understanding martial arts, to healing a fraught sibling relationship and possibly, in some ways, even how I think about men.

I have two brothers but the brother closest in age was a 'frenemy'. We would play beautifully for snatches but as we got older we increasingly fought – violently, loudly and mercilessly. I was constantly annoyed by his exuberance, his ever-ready energy and what I saw as his aggression. I then went off to an all-girls high school and boys become a mystery until they became an obsession. Since then, my male mates and my husband have taught me a terrific amount about being a bloke, but seeing a son grow up is giving me a cellular, visceral and emotional understanding.

My son looks a lot like the brother I battled. He even talks, walks and acts in a manner that transports me back to being nine years old. I can see myself in his older sister as she slams the bedroom door in his pleading face. I feel his hurt at the rejection so deeply I wish I could rewind time to apologise to his uncle. I now understand what happens on the other side of that door; the sweetness and vulnerability of the boy that battles.

While my daughter lives in an imaginary world of her own creation, my son is firmly grounded on earth. I can see his body constantly craving excitement, sensation and physicality; hence the tackling, hugging, hitting and whacking of friends and his family. While I used to be furious at my brother for picking up and wielding every stick he saw and destroying every single toy we had, I see my son as a physical entity making sense of the world with his body. I feel my daughter's pain at the consequences but realise she usually gives as good as she gets. Perhaps I've edited my own violence out of my story.

My son's need for physical sensations even wake him most nights. He still comes into our bedroom, so I wake nearly daily to the brush of his soft warm cheek and puffs of tiny breath inches from my face.

His non-verbal communication is another understanding he's given me about boys. While he's often a chatty young thing, my son doesn't need to talk about everything. In fact, when he's most emotional, the verbal part of his brain shuts down. His first sentence at age three was 'Mum, just stop talking!' Sometimes, less really is more.

While my daughter can fool me rather easily, my son is more transparent when he's been naughty. His body betrays him; a tight twist to his mouth, his long lashed eyes cast to the side and shoulders hunched. When I ask, 'What have you done?' he'll reply, 'Nothing, but don't look under my bed.' When I then find the party animal or diary he's stolen from his sister, he's astonished by his inability at subterfuge.

There's also purity in his passion. My son loves music. As do all his mates. They dance rapturously; connecting with a primal, deep, beautiful and spiritual rhythm. I pray the day never comes when they get self-conscious and resort to the Aussie white-boy shuffle. The girls sing to hairbrushes and do their jazz ballet – but for the boys, the music is glue that binds them to one another and to their bodies. They absorb it totally, recklessly and powerfully. They meet in its beats as their bodies meet in space.

I see my son's friendships, forged on the dance floor and the martial arts hall, in all their glory. I am coming to understand the visceral need boys have to belong. I've always bristled at the word 'gang' but now feel my son's desire to bond; his band of brothers feel confident and secure in their unity and they love each other deeply.

I once heard a male educator say humour is a great way to connect with boys. He's right. My son may not need to talk but he frequently needs to laugh. He has a fabulous sense of the ridiculousness in life and doesn't always try to make sense of it. I can see the male sense of humour forming and I honour it as much as his tears of pain. Perhaps this generation of young men, far less likely to be told 'stop crying, boys don't cry', will keep showing that vulnerability.

While hearing my son's glorious giggle and watching him negotiate the rigours of school and a world of complications, I ache for his vulnerable spirit. I can now see my brother's softness, bruised heart and good nature. And at times, I find it easier to see the boy in other men. As a bonus, my brother has had a little girl. It's beautiful to watch him begin a journey of understanding from the other side.

Now it's time for the journey of this book to come to an end. It's kind of sad to finish our conversation. So just one rather large thing to end with.

Most books on 'parenting' have a built-in assumption, never named but always there – that that the world we live in is just fine, and our job is to fit our kids into it well. That the procession of human life is headed to a golden, prosperous future, and we only need to keep our kids from falling by the wayside. Perhaps (though this is not usually stated), we can help them push to the head of the queue.

Of course, this is a massive lie. The very best science and knowledge is that we live in a time of dystopian collapse, where inequality, the misuse of resources, and above all the crisis of climate change will lead to disrupted agriculture, famine, mass migration and war. We know this because it's already begun.

It's almost certain that our kids will live in far worse times than we have, and our grandchildren may not be able to live at all. We don't need kids who fit in. We need *heroes* – young men and women who are strong-hearted, caring, calm and passionate and have a purpose beyond themselves – to care for the whole species and the life that sustains it. To turn things around. To promote radical, non-violent change. We need good men and women in numbers like never before. That's what we have aimed to raise at our house, and we hope you will too.

In love and hope,
Steve Biddulph

Notes

BOYHOOD HAS CHANGED
1. Fletcher, Richard, *Australian Men and Boys: A Picture of Health?*, Department of Health Studies, University of Newcastle, 1995.

CHAPTER 2: THE THREE STAGES OF BOYHOOD
1. Breastfeeding babies provides them with nutrients which especially stimulate brain development. These nutrients are not currently present in formula milks. Battin, D.A., Marrs, R.P., Fleiss, P.M., Mishell, D.R. Jr (1985), 'Effect of suckling on serum prolactin, luteinizing hormone, follicle-stimulating hormone, and estradiol during prolonged lactation', *Obstet Gynecol.*, June, 65, 6, 785–88.
2. Phillips, Angela, *The Trouble with Boys*, Pandora, London, 1993.
3. University of Washington psychologist Geraldine Dawson found that depressed mothers raised babies with abnormally low levels of brain activity. If the mother rose above her depression to lavish care and energy on the baby, the baby recovered. Also, if the mother recovered before the baby was one year old, then the baby completely recovered. If neither of these things happened, the child acquired a 'sad brain' permanently. Reported in Nash, J.M., 'Fertile Minds', in *Time*, 3 February 1997.
4. Greenspan, S., and Rolfe, S, cited in *Motherhood, How should we care for our children?*, Manne, A., Allen and Unwin, 2007. See also *Why Love Matters, how affection shapes a baby's brain*, Gerhardt, S., Brunner Routledge, NY, 2004.
5. Gurian, Michael, *The Wonder of Boys*, Tarcher/Putnam, New York, 1996. Gurian puts more weight than I would on the effects of testosterone, suggesting that it dominates a boy's psychology above all else. He advocates sometimes smacking boys (somehow not making the connection that this invariably makes them more violent). Apart from these concerns, his book has many good points and has been influential for a more positive view of boys.
6. Silverstein, Olga, and Rashbaum, Beth, *The Courage to Raise Good Men*, Penguin, Melbourne, 1994.
7. This kind of socialisation of males is brilliantly depicted in several films, including *The Remains of the Day* starring Anthony Hopkins and *The Browning Version* with Albert Finney.
8. 'HSC robs young. There's more to life than exam results, Deane warns students' in the *Daily Telegraph*, 10 February, 1997, page 17. Former Governor-General Sir William Deane told a parent group: 'It is … essential that schools students and parents keep a proper sense of proportion and pay due regard to the importance of community service, growing political awareness, cultural pursuits, social contacts and the sheer enjoyment of life.'
9. At birth, testosterone levels are soaring at 250 mg/ml. From five to ten years of age, testosterone levels in the blood are as low as 30 mg/ml. At fifteen, they reach 600 mg/ml, which is the full adult level. From Semple, Michael, 'How to live forever', *Esquire*, September 1993, page 127. Also Dow, S., 'Hormone new hope for flagging males', *The Age*, 19 May 1995, p. 11 reports that testosterone affects the frequency of sexual

behaviour; and Dabbs, J.M. (1995), 'Testosterone, crime and misbehaviour among male prison inmates', *Journal of Personality and Individual Differences* 18:5, 627–33, shows a strong link between testosterone levels and behavioural problems in prisons.

10. Smith, Babette, *Mothers and Sons*, Allen & Unwin, Sydney, 1995, p. 20.

11. Tierney, J.P., Grossman, J.B. and Resch, N. (1995), 'Making a difference: an impact study of big brothers/big sisters (BB/BS)', Public/Private Ventures, Philadelphia, PA.

12. Sax, Leonard, *Why Gender Matters*, Broadway Books, New York, 2005.

13. Caine, Janel (1991), 'The effects of music on selected stress behaviours, weight, caloric and formula intake and length of hospital stay of premature and low birthweight neonates in a newborn intensive care unit', *Journal of Music Therapy*, 28, 180–92. See also Cone Wesson, Barbara et al. (1997), 'Hearing sensitivity in newborns estimated from ABRs to bone conducted sounds', *Journal of the American Academy of Audiology* 8, 299–307.

14. A rather damning rebuttal of Dr Sax's conclusions on hearing is given by Linguistics Professor Mark Liberman in his Language Log blog of 22 August 2006, also cited in the *New York Times*, http://itre.cis.upenn.edu/~myl/languagelog/archives/003487.html, or just google Liberman Language Log.

15. Rowe, K., Pollard J., 'Literacy, behaviour and auditory processing: Does teacher professional development make a difference?', background paper to Rue Wright Memorial Award presented at the Royal Australasian College of Physicians Scientific Meeting, Wellington, New Zealand, 2005. Their advice, in a nutshell, was that teachers can hugely improve the literacy and general learning of boys, especially with some simple measures learned in a one-hour seminar. 'Salient elements ... included consciousness raising and training in the following classroom-based strategies: (1) Attract the child's attention; speak slowly, use short sentences ('chunked'), maintain eye contact, use visual cues and wait for compliance; (2) Pause between sentences. If repeats are required, restate slowly and simply, and provide regular encouragement; Monitor the child; e.g., if 'blank look' response, stop and begin instruction again; Establish hearing, listening and compliance routines.'

CHAPTER 3: TESTOSTERONE

1. Donovan, B.T., *Hormones and Human Behaviour: The Scientific Basis of Psychiatry*, CUP, Cambridge, 1985. Also Fausto-Sterling, A., *Myths of Gender*, Basic Books, New York, 1985.

2. Guatelli-Steinbergy, D., Boyce, J., 'The postnatal endocrine surge and its effects on subsequent sexual growth' in Preedy, V.R. (ed.), *Handbook of Growth and Growth Monitoring in Health and Disease*, Springer, New York, 2012, pp. 663–81.

3. Schore, A.N. (2017), 'All our sons: the developmental neurobiology and neuroendocrinology of boys at risk', *Infant Ment Health J.*, Jan, 38, 1, 15–52. DOI: 10.1002/imhj.21616. Epub 2017 Jan 2.

4. Gerhardt, Sue, *Why Love Matters*, Routledge, London, 2004.

5. A 2014 editorial in *Hormones and Behavior* signed by twenty journal editors-in-chief and twenty-eight journal associate editors declared, 'Thousands of published studies have revealed the health effects of endocrine disrupting chemicals on wildlife and laboratory animals and, moreover, have shown associations of endocrine disrupting chemicals with effects in humans ... Of particular concern is incontrovertible evidence ... that there are critical life stages, especially during early development, when hormones dictate the differentiation and development of tissues. Any perturbation of the delicate hormonal balance, whether due to the absence of natural hormones or presence of exogenous hormones, can have irreversible effects on endocrine-sensitive organs. Endocrine disrupting chemicals are known to upset the balance' (Gore et al., 2014, p. 190).

In a position statement in endocrinology, authors offered recommendations for strengthening the Endocrine Disruptor Screening Program (Zoeller et al., 2012), and in *Lancet Neurology*, Grandjean and Landrigan (2014) called for an urgent formation of an international clearing house. Writing in *Annual Review of Public Health*, Lanphear (2015) argued, 'The optimal strategy to prevent the development of brain-based disorders is to identify and restrict or ban the use of potential toxins before they are marketed or discharged into the environment' (p. 222).

6. 'Throughout this work, I have provided evidence that the brain development of the male fetus, infant, and boy is slower than that of its female counterparts, and thereby more at risk. According to Zahn-Waxler et al. (2008) "The curve of development of the frontal cortex, caudate, and temporal lobes in girls is considerably faster than in boys, by as much as 20 months" (p. 279). At ages 7 to 12, boys lag behind girls by as much as 2 years in the development of social sensitivity (Baron-Cohen, O'Riordan, Jones, Stone and Plaisted, 1999.' Schore, A.N. (2017), 'All our sons: the developmental neurobiology and neuroendocrinology of boys at risk', *Infant Ment Health J.*, Jan, 38, 1, 15–52. DOI: 10.1002/imhj.21616. Epub 2017 Jan 2.

7. Mitamura, R., Yano, K., Suzuki, N., Y., Makita, Y., Okuno, A. (1999), 'Diurnal rhythms of luteinizing hormone, follicle-stimulating hormone, and testosterone secretion before the onset of male puberty', *The Journal of Clinical Endocrinology & Metabolism*, 84, 1, 29–37. https://doi.org/10.1210/jcem.84.1.5404.

8. Steinbeck, K., 'Health Check: do boys really have a testosterone spurt at age four?', *The Conversation*, 23 October 2017.

9. Mundy, L.K., Romaniuk, H., et al., (2015), 'Adrenarche and the emotional and behavioral problems of late childhood', *J Adolesc Health*, 57, 6, 608–16, DOI: 10.1016/j. jadohealth.2015.09.001; Byrne, Michelle L., Whittle, Sarah et al. (2017), 'A systematic review of adrenarche as a sensitive period in neurobiological development and mental health', *Developmental Cognitive Neuroscience* 25, 12–28.

10. https://www.mcri.edu.au/news/early-puberty-hormones-increase-emotional-and-behavioural-issues-boys: Murdoch Children Research Institute Newsletter, 22 November 2015; Byrne, M.L. et al. (2017), 'A systematic review of adrenarche as a sensitive period in neurobiological development and mental health', *Dev Cogn Neurosci*, Jun, 25, 12–28. DOI: 10.1016/j.dcn.2016.12.004. Epub 2016 Dec 21.

11. Senserrick, T. and Whelan, M. (2003), 'Graduated driver licensing: Effectiveness of systems and individual components', Monash University Accident Research Centre Report #209. A good summary of the research argument for passenger restrictions for P plate drivers is at http://www.walk.com.au/pedestriancouncil/Page. asp?PageID=1982.

12. The long-term studies of testosterone levels and hierarchical behaviour in a community of monkeys was carried out by Robert Rose, Department of Psychiatry, Walter Reed Army Institute of Research, Washington, cited in Bahr, Robert, *The Virility Factor*, Longman, New York, 1976.

13. Elium, D. and Elium, J., *Raising a Son: Parents and the Making of a Healthy Man*, Beyond Words, Oregon, 1992.

14. The observation of boys behaving well in Montessori schools was first pointed out by Peter Vogel at the NSW Federation of P and C Associations forum on boys in schools, February 1997.

15. Reported by Dr Rex Stoessiger in Hobart. Personal communication, May 1997.

CHAPTER 4: MAKING A NEW KIND OF MAN

1. There is no better introduction to the importance of vulnerability than Brene Brown's world famous TED talk, as well as her books on the subject. She points out that everything worthwhile in life – love, closeness, adventure, creativity, fun, and change – all require us to be vulnerable. https://www.ted.com/talks/brene_brown_on_vulnerability

2. Lashley, C., *Journey to Prison: Who Goes and Why?*, HarperCollins, Australia, 2002.

3. Hollier, L. P., Maybery, M., Keelan, J., Hickey, M. and Whitehouse, A. (2014), 'Perinatal testosterone exposure and cerebral lateralisation in adult males: Evidence for the callosal hypothesis', *Biological Psychology*, 103, 1, 48–53. DOI: 10.1016/j.

biopsycho.2014.08.009. Males exposed to the highest testosterone levels were more than twice as likely to have a language delay at age three. In addition to the language deficits, males were more likely to be classified as having delays in fine-motor function (11 per cent versus 6.4 per cent) and personal-social skills (25.3 per cent versus 14.3 per cent); Whitehouse A. et al. (2012), 'Sex-specific associations between umbilical cord blood testosterone levels and language delay in early childhood', *J Child Psychol Psychiatry.* DOI: 10.1111/j.1469-7610.2011.02523.x.

4. There is currently some debate about this widespread finding, as to whether boys are more often diagnosed with a learning difficulty due to their tendency to behave unacceptably when frustrated with not being able to learn well at school. Some studies find that if girls and boys are assessed objectively, the difference is not so great: Coutinho, M.J. and Oswald, D.P. (2005), 'State variation in gender disproportionality in special education: Finding and recommendations', *Remedial and Special Education*, 26, 1, 7–15; Bandian, N. A. (1999), 'Reading disability defined as a discrepancy between listening and reading comprehension: A longitudinal study of stability, gender differences, and prevalence', *Journal of Learning Disabilities*, 32, 2, 138–48.

CHAPTER 5: WHAT DADS CAN DO

1. Burgess, Adrienne, *Fatherhood Reclaimed*, Vermillion, London, 1997. Burgess noted the beginning of this trend in the mid-90s, and it was being confirmed ten years later. See also Bennett, R., 'Children never had it so good', *The Times*, 4 October 2006 and for more detail, see the original report, Future Foundation Report, The Changing Face of Parenting, 2007. www.futurefoundation.net

2. Paul Whyte, Sydney Men's Network, at 'Boys in Education' seminar, Hobart, 1994.

3. Biddulph, S. and Biddulph, S., *The Making of Love*, Doubleday, Sydney, 1989.

4. Copyright © 1992 by Jack Kammer. Jack Kammer is the author of *Good Will Toward Men*, St Martin's Press, New York, 1995.

5. Blankenhorn. D., *Fatherless America*, Basic Books, New York, 1995. Blankenhorn's book makes a powerful case, especially for the US, where 40 per cent of children do not have their father in the home. Low attainment at school, teen pregnancy, juvenile crime convictions, learning difficulties and early school-leaving, as well as domestic violence and sexual abuse of children, are all higher in families where the birth father is no longer present. Single mothers and lesbian couples can raise children well, but those who do best are aware of and do their best to meet the need for same-sex role models for their sons.

6. Dr Gordon Serfontein, who pioneered the concept of ADD in Australia, writes in *The Hidden Handicap: How to Help Children Who Suffer from Dyslexia, Hyperactivity, and Learning Difficulties* (Simon and Schuster, Australia, 1998) that the absence of fathers is a component in the problems associated with ADD. He urges fathers to get involved in playing with, and teaching self-control to their sons. Also worth reading is Gardner, N., *A Friend Like Henry*, Hodder & Stoughton, London 2007. The book is about the role of a dog in helping overcome autism, but to the reader its clear that both parents working as a team was central to this moving and positive outcome.

7. Biddulph, S., *Manhood*, Finch, Australia, 2005.

8. Maggie Dent, personal communication, December 2017.

CHAPTER 6: MOTHERS AND SONS

1. The failure of as many as 30 per cent of students in their first year of university has attracted some concern; findings include poor teaching skills in university staff, and the benefit of good transition programmes. The personal attributes of students appear to matter more than raw ability. This maturity factor makes a good argument for the growing use of a gap year or two after secondary school. Evans, M., (2000) 'Planning for the transition to tertiary study: A literature review' (Monash University Research Paper).

2. Gurian, Michael, *The Wonder of Boys*, Tarcher/Putnam, New York, 1996.
3. Wilcox, B., et al., Report of the APA Taskforce on Advertizing and Children 2004: http://www.apa.org/pubs/info/reports/advertising-children.aspx
4. Seligman, M., *Learned Optimism*, Random House, Sydney, 1992, p. 84.

CHAPTER 7: DEVELOPING A HEALTHY SEXUALITY

1. Generally around 80 per cent of young males report a frequency of five times a week or more in confidential surveys. This appears to be cross-cultural, and today is seen by medical authorities as emotionally healthy and physically beneficial unless very excessive. Heilborn, M.L., Cabral, C.S. (2006), 'Sexual practices in youth', *Cadernos de Saúde Pública* 22, 7, Instituto de Medicina Social, Universidade do Estado do Rio de Janeiro, Brazil.
2. Bly, Robert, *The Sibling Society*, Heinemann, Australia, 1996.
3. Jensen, R., *The End of Patriarchy*, Spinifex Press, Australia, 2017.
4. http://www.latimes.com/opinion/op-ed/la-oe-soh-trans-feminism-anti-science-20170210-story.html
5. Dr Bernadette Wren, quoted in McCann, C., 'When girls won't be girls', *Economist*, 28 September 2017, https://www.1843magazine.com/features/when-girls-wont-be-girls. This article gives both for and against arguments with an in-depth account of a young person's own experience transitioning and de-transitioning.
6. https://www.theguardian.com/society/2016/feb/26/crucial-study-transgender-children-mental-health-family-support; de Cuypere, G., T'Sjoen, G., Beerten, R. et al. (2005), 'Sexual and physical health after sex reassignment surgery', *Arch Sex Behav.* 34, 679–90; Dhejne, C., Lichtenstein, P., Boman, M., Johansson, A. L. V., Långström, N., Landén, M. (2011), 'Long-term follow-up of transsexual persons undergoing sex reassignment surgery: Cohort Study in Sweden', *PLoS One*, 2011, 6.
7. Cited in http://www.independent.co.uk/life-style/health-and-families/features/what-the-critics-say-about-treatment-for-transgender-children-a7377851.html.
8. Wood, H. (2011), 'The internet and its role in the escalation of sexually compulsive behaviour', *Psychoanalytic Psychotherapy*, 25, 2, 127–42.
9. Bernard, P., Gervais, S.J. et al. (2012), 'Integrating Sexual Objectification with object versus person recognition', *Psychological Science*, April 2012, 469–71.
10. Wood, H. (2011), 'The Internet and its role in the escalation of sexually compulsive behaviour', *Psychoanalytic Psychotherapy*, 25, 2, 127–42.
11. Greenfield, S., 'How digital culture is rewiring our brains', *Sydney Morning Herald*, 7 August 2012.
12. Clark, Elizabeth, *Love, Sex and No Regrets for Today's Teens*, Finch, Sydney, 2017.
13. Biddulph, S., *Manhood*, Finch, Australia, 2005.
14. In 'Being gay is a big factor in youth suicides', Debra Jopson (*Sydney Morning Herald*, 26 February 1997) referred to the large-scale research of Dr Gary Remafedi at the University of Minnesota, which found that 30 per cent of gay adolescent boys said they had tried to kill themselves. Risk factors were 'coming out' at an early age, substance abuse and displaying behaviour considered effeminate.
15. Black, D, Gates, G., Sanders, S., Taylor, L. (2000), 'Demographics of the gay and lesbian population in the United States: Evidence from available systematic data sources', *Demography*, 37, 2 (May, 2000), 139–54 (available on JSTOR). See also Hite, S., *The Hite Report on Male Sexuality*, New York, A. Knopf, 1991.
16. http://www.pewinternet.org/2008/09/16/part-1-1-who-is-playing-games/
17. Gentile, D.A., Bailey,K., et al. (2017), 'Internet Gaming Disorder in Children and Adolescents', *Pediatrics* 140 (Supplement 2), S81-S85; DOI: 10.1542/peds.2016-1758H.
18. LeBourgeois, M.K., et al. (2017), 'Digital Media and Sleep in Childhood and Adolescence', *Pediatrics*, 140 (Supplement 2), S92–S96; DOI: 10.1542/peds.2016-1758J.
19. Robinson, T.N., Banda, J.A, et al. (2017), 'Screen Media Exposure and Obesity in Children and Adolescents', *Pediatrics* 140 (Supplement 2, S97–S101; DOI: 10.1542/peds.2016-1758K.

20. Anderson, C.A., Warburton, W., et al. (2017), 'Screen Violence and Youth Behavior', *Pediatrics* 140 (Supplement 2), S142–S147; DOI: 10.1542/peds.2016-1758T.

CHAPTER 8: OUT INTO THE BIG WORLD

1. Biddulph, S., *Raising Babies: Should Under 3s Go to Nursery?*, Thorsons, London, 2006.

2. Vann, A. S. (1991), 'Let's not push our kindergarten kids', *Education Digest* 57, 4.3. Also Cratty, B.J., *Perceptual Motor Development in Infants and Children*, Prentice Hall, New Jersey, 1986. 'Sex-related differences in motor development are present as early as the preschool years. Boys are slightly advanced over girls in abilities that emphasise force and power. Girls have an edge in fine-motor skills of drawing and penmanship and in certain gross-motor capacities that combine balance and foot movement such as hopping and skipping. Girls are ahead of boys in overall physical maturity, which may be partly responsible for their better balance and precision of movement. Only in mid–late teens do boys catch up with girls. At this age, boys increase in speed, strength and endurance athletically, until even the average boy outperforms most girls.'

   Hellinck, Walter-Grietens (1994), 'Competence and behavioral problems in six- to twelve-year-old children in Flanders (Belgium)', *Journal of Emotional & Behavioural Disorders*, 2, 130: 'The typical girl is slightly shorter than the typical boy at all ages until adolescence. She becomes taller shortly after age 11 because her adolescent spurt takes place two years earlier than the boy's. At age 14 she is surpassed again in height by the typical boy.

   'Girls obtained significantly higher scores on all competence items and sub-scales on which sex differences were found, and also on Total Competence. Sex differences in competence may be a reflection of developmental and maturation differences between boys and girls, particularly in acquiring cognitive and social skills to perform well in school' (Berk, 1989; Kogan, 1983; Minuchin & Shapiro, 1983).

   'No sex differences in standard developmental milestones – sitting up, walking, grasping. Girls begin talking earlier and language problems occur far more in males (boys outnumber girls in remedial reading classes by 4:1). Male foetus more likely to abort, higher rate of congenital defects and anoxia. Greater male vulnerability – shift from female to male developmental pattern increases chances of mishap or females have extra genetic protection with respect to any aspect of development affected by gene on the X chromosome.' 29 January, © 1996 Deseret News Publishing Co., Lecture 7: 'Sex or gender?'

3. In addition, the structured nature of learning now in vogue as pre-schools style themselves as 'Early Learning Centres' is proving counter-productive. A strong consensus among child development experts is that formal learning should not commence until around age 6. See for example Bruton, C., 'Do we send our children to school too young?' *The Times*, 6 September 2007. See also a National Foundation for Educational Research Review of Primary Education, summarised in Woolcock, N., 'Children "Too young for school at 4"', *The Times*, 8 February 2008.

4. The figures are slightly higher in the US, slightly lower for the UK and Australia. See Blankenhorn. D., *Fatherless America*, Basic Books, New York, 1995 for the US and Adrienne Burgess, *Fatherhood Reclaimed*, Vermillion, London, 1997 for the UK.

5. The tendency of male teachers to get 'hormonally' stirred up when teaching boys who threaten them has an amusing parallel in work with primates: 'Adolescent male chimps in the facility test recruits by spitting water, banging on cages and similar stunts. Deborah Fouts reports that women survive the initiation at a rate of 3 to 1 over men because women ignore the antics, while men tend to be get impatient, react to the provocation, and escalate the chimps' rampages.' Reported in Vines, G., *Raging Hormones*, Virago Press, London, 1993.

6. Stoessiger, R., 'Boys and Literacy – an equity issue', accessible at Manhood Online website: http://www.manhood.com.au.

7. Hudson, M. and Carr, L., 'Ending Alienation', *The Gen*, June 1966.
8. Rigby, K., *Bullying in Schools and What to do About it*, ACER, Canberra, 1996. See also http://www.education.unisa.edu.au/bullying/childtelus.htm.
9. Adapted from Rigby, *Bullying Schools and What to Do About It*, ibid.
10. Ireland, Peter, *Boys in Schools*, Fletcher & Browne, Finch Publishing, Sydney, 1995.
11. Dunaif-Hattis, J., 'Doubling the brain: on the evolution of brain lateralisation and its implications for language', cited in *Grolier's Encyclopedia*.
12. This was in the early 1990s. The situation has improved: by 2005 the difference was 77 per cent of girls and 60 per cent of boys, although taking only the A and B scores, it was 50–30 per cent respectively. http://news.bbc.co.uk/2/shared/bsp/hi/education/05/exam_results/gcse_fc/html/art.stm
13. 'Mid-school Crisis', *Sydney Morning Herald*, 17 February 1997, p. 12.
14. Biddulph, S., *The New Manhood*, Finch, Australia, 2013.
15. This list was devised by Deborah Hartman and Richard Fletcher, Boys to Fine Men Program, University of Newcastle, NSW. To learn more about this program, visit: www.newcastle.edu.au/centre/fac/boys/aboutusb/htm
16. White, Darren (1992), 'What is it like to be autistic?', *Autism Spectrum Disorder*, Autistic Association of NSW, Sydney.

CHAPTER 9: BOYS AND SPORT

1. Messner, Michael, *Power at Play: Sports and the Problem of Masculinity*, Beacon Press, Boston, 1992.
2. Lecture to Men's Health and Wellbeing Association (NSW) Open Day, Sydney, November 1996.
3. *Sydney Morning Herald*, 12 June 2007. See also Finch, C., Valuri, G., and Ozanne Smith, J., (2012), 'Sport and active recreation injuries in Australia: evidence from emergency department presentations', *British Journal of Sports Medicine* 32, 3, 220–25; Spinks, A., Macpherson. A., Bain, C., McClure, C. (2006), 'Injury risk from popular childhood physical activities: results from an Australian primary school cohort', *Injury Prevention* 12, 390–94; http://www.abc.net.au/news/2016-11-15/australian-children-needing-knee-surgery-for-sports-injuries/8008236

CHAPTER 10: A COMMUNITY CHALLENGE

1. Polanczyk G., de Lima, M.S., Horta, B.L., Biederman J., Rohde, L. A. (2007), 'The worldwide prevalence of ADHD: a systematic review and metaregression analysis', *Am J Psychiatry* 164, 6, 942–8.
2. Mate, G., *Scattered, How Attention Deficit Disorder Originates, and What You Can Do About It*, Plume, New York, 2000. The Pediatric Advisory Committee of the Food and Drug Administration released a statement on 30 June 2005 identifying two possible safety concerns regarding Concerta, Ritalin and other brands of methylphenidate: psychiatric adverse effects and cardiovascular adverse effects. The best hands-on guidebook for helping ADHD children in the home and the classroom, as recommended by Gabor Mate (though he disagrees with the title), is Thomas Armstrong's *The Myth of the ADD Child: 50 Ways to Improve Your Child's Behavior and Attention Span without Drugs, Labels, or Coercion*, Plume, New York, 1997. This is a very practical book about non-drug methods to help ADHD children learn to focus and calm down, at home and in the classroom.
3. Lunn, S., 'Teenage drink and drug abuse rife', *The Australian*, 25 February 2008. 'Overall among 12- to 17-year-olds, one in 10 (168,000) report binge-drinking (defined as seven or more standard drinks in a day for a male and five or more standard drinks for a female), in any given week. For 16-year-olds, the figure is one in five (54,116), the same as for 17-year-olds (59,176). For young indigenous Australians, 27 per cent use alcohol and 12 per cent drink to excess. Of particular concern is the finding that approximately 13 per cent of young drinkers report drink-driving and 16 per cent report going to work or school under the influence of alcohol,' the report finds.

The problem is compounded by how many young people live with a parent who binge drinks or uses cannabis on a daily basis: 'The Federal Government's principal advisory body on drugs policy said its estimates last May about the disturbing number of children exposed to adult binge-drinkers and cannabis users had proven to be significantly short of the mark. A reassessment of the research finds almost double the numbers, estimating that 451,000 children are exposed to binge drinking and that 70,000 live with a daily cannabis user.'

4. Hinsliff, G., 'Parents to face court over young drinkers', *Observer*, 1 June, 2008.
5. Chromosome abnormalities were discovered in a small-scale investigation that has not yet been validated by a large-scale controlled study. 'Cytogenetic effects in children treated with methylphenidate', *Cancer Letters*, 18 December 2005, 230, 2. The study suggested that further research is warranted considering the established link between chromosome aberrations and cancer, and considering that all the children in this study showed suspicious DNA changes within a very short time. Dr David Jacobson-Kram of the FDA said that while the study had flaws in its methods, its results could not be dismissed.

Do Gender Differences Exist, and Do They Matter?

The science, and the subtlety, of raising kids to be equal

For most readers, the idea of biological gender differences is not problematic. They take a middle view – that gender is a factor, but not a deciding factor – in who our kids are and how to raise them well.

Occasionally though, someone takes issue with the very idea of treating the genders differently. (Or having books addressing one gender or the other.) In part I would agree. Children are children, and much of parenting is the same regardless of a child's sex.

But should we always treat kids the same regardless of whether they are a boy or girl? There was a widespread social project from the 1970s onwards to reduce differences in childrearing so that kids could be free to be themselves. My books don't dispute this – in fact they support it. Boys doing cooking and housework is one of the key messages of *Raising Boys*; girls being loud, messy, wild and strong is a notable theme of *Ten Things Girls Need Most*. I am arguably the leading advocate in the world for parents playing an equal role in childrearing. I am clear that every girl and boy should be raised to be a feminist (and have had men's rights' chaps shout at me for saying this).

But my books also say something else – that *it's not enough* to treat kids the same. We also have to work specifically to address the risk factors of being a boy or girl that in the twenty-first century are still very much in evidence. Boys are nine times more likely to go to jail, far more likely to rape, commit suicide or die in a car crash. And much less likely to go to university. Girls are far more likely to self-harm, to suffer from depression, and so on.

Even if you subscribe to the idea that there are no innate gender continua along which all kids are biologically located (i.e. you believe that it's all down to conditioning), this point still holds. Most kids today are still very gendered (even though some are finding a place between those extremes). So we have to address that, especially when it's limiting, or harmful to their lives or those around them. The big question is how. Gender-blind childrearing was one attempt, and in childcare centres, schools and enlightened homes, this began in earnest forty years ago and continues to this day.

By the 1990s though, it was clear that this project was not progressing as it should, especially with improving boys' behaviour and their ability to relate well to women and girls. Arguably, things were getting worse. And then in the 2000s we began to see a serious decline in the mental health of girls. This too was gender-specific and needed unique answers. And, quietly in the background, all through those decades, we learnt more and more about gender on a cellular, biochemical and structural level, which pointed to the whole question being far more complex than originally thought.

Let's give an example. One of the most persistent and important differences between boys and girls is in their ability to read. Boys are three times more likely to struggle with reading, and overall are worse readers throughout their school lives. This has long been a problem, and very recent research shows that it is not going away.[1] Even in the most advanced education systems such as those of Finland and Scandinavia, girls remain better readers than boys. And as cited earlier, brain differences seem to be at the heart of this. The higher a boy's testosterone levels *in utero*, the poorer a reader he seems to be for life. So our efforts have to be redoubled and refocused to reduce that difference, since it limits and harms boys, but also makes them less able to communicate well with girls or understand their own feelings and choices. Parents need to know that reading to their boys is vital – it humanises them and helps them be better people. Even if they never catch up with most girls, we can't just let things be.

On a wider front, the slower development of most boys, cognitively and physically (not in size, but in motor control) adds to the problem. They very often find the formal nature of schooling to be acutely stressful. Forced into sit-down schooling too young, they grow to dislike school, behave badly and learn less well. Their life chances are reduced. It is a serious risk factor (most men in prison did terribly at school). It has a biological origin. And if we know about it we can work to prevent it.[2]

It's not only boys who are affected when we fail to take gender differences into account. Leading girls' educator JoAnn Deak[3] points out that girls face a danger here too. Because they are better thinkers, and more willing to sit still, they are seen as 'good' at school in the early years. These girls attract much praise and affirmation from parents and teachers. But this can lead to girls orientating themselves to praise from adults, rather than learning for its own sake. They become 'pleasers' and are shaped towards being tidy, compliant and approval-seeking in their approach to learning. Since we now have serious mental health issues arising from perfectionism and overachieving in girls, this clearly harms them as well.

There are hundreds of small but impactful factors like this – not just between boys and girls, but within the genders too, which cascade into their life chances. Most boys tend to be larger and stronger when they are young and when they are adults (there is a window in the early teens when girls are bigger than boys). And so being specifically trained to be gentle and not use physical domination needs to be a part of boys' upbringing and socialisation – with school programmes etc. that teach and model positive masculinities.

Hormones are the way that gender is mediated in the bodies of all animals including human beings. They lead to what is called gender dimorphism – different body shapes, organs, as well as brain structures and behavioural traits. My favourite is the elephant seal: the females are a hefty 300 kg, but the males an astonishing ten times larger – 3 tonnes. It's a very lucky break that in humans, our ecological niche required us to be actually very similar. Women needed to be able to throw a spear, and men to raise a baby. So we haven't so far to go towards equality. Feminism will be a long time coming to elephant seals.

In the economical way of nature, sometimes the same hormones – such as luteinising hormone – are used for completely different purposes in boys and girls. Hormones are not simple, but that does not mean we can ignore them. Testosterone does not cause aggression, but in combination with the stress hormone cortisol it can make aggression more likely when the conditions are right. Even within the genders, kids differ enormously in their individual levels of these hormones. No two boys or girls are alike. But we can still mitigate the effects reliably. Secure, well-loved and empathically raised boys and men are rarely aggressive. Knowing about that risk can make us doubly determined to help our boys, especially those who have more masculinised bodies and brains, to be thoughtful, caring, and safe.

Again, it's important to see the subtleties. It's recently been found that absolute testosterone levels are not as significant as a change in the level, which can result from situations of loss or exclusion, even momentarily. Male human beings are far more susceptible to shame – most find it more toxic even than physical pain. This is strongly believed to be linked to evolutionary factors.[4] A boy doesn't need to be top of the pack, but he needs to feel part of the pack. It's the exclusion that he feels to be life-threatening. And so we have to work with at-risk boys to find better roles, and better ways to belong. (Once in a youth group I helped to run, we had a number of burglaries at our hall. Having a fair idea of which boy was responsible, we asked him to keep an eye on the venue for us. He would visit it at night to make sure it was locked and safe. Problem solved.)

What you were taught in university is not what we now know is true. If you studied social science in the 1970s you would have likely been told that there are more variations within the genders than there are between them. That might impress a first year tutorial group, but it is both a grammatical and a statistical nonsense. You can't compare two variable groups except by comparing the average or the mean for those groups. And if those averages differ, you have lost your case. (Fish vary from minnows to whale sharks, but that doesn't make them people.) We can only compare by separate traits. So in IQ there is no difference, other than that more males are at the extremes. But in upper body strength, or tallness, men predominate. Girls begin puberty sooner and get it over much faster. Boys have hormonal changes at four, and again at eight, girls normally do not. And it has very different effects on their bodies. And so on.

The other simple idea often taught was that sex is what you are born with, and gender what you are given. No serious scientist today thinks it's possible to separate those – they interact in infinitely complex ways, as Cordelia Fine argues beautifully in her book *Testosterone Rex*.[5] We have largely given up using the word gender to indicate what is purely cultural. When young people decide they are transgender, it's their actual bodies that they want to change, not their conditioning.

Those who argue for ignoring gender often cite Cordelia's earlier book *Delusions of Gender*,[6] usually without having properly read it. Her stance is not that gender is a delusion, but that some rather silly generalisations have occurred in its name. Nobody I know is arguing with that; we are not from separate planets. But *Delusions* has a separate problem: it is far from being the mainstream view of neuroscientists. Brain science is a huge field, with a body of knowledge that is intensely scrutinised and peer reviewed, and its practitioners are acutely aware of the risks of sexism. A number of leading voices[7] have taken its author to task for skirting over the hundreds of known differences on a molecular, cellular, and structural level in the human brain, between most boys, and most girls.[8]

That may well be why Cordelia wrote *Testosterone Rex* six years later. Like *Delusions*, it's a lively read and I highly recommend it. But at the same time, it suffered one flaw – the book's cover conveys a somewhat different message to its actual conclusions. It's hard not to suspect that the further the author got into the material, the more complicated the picture grew. She concludes, in the end, that, 'Sex does indeed matter, but in a complicated and unpredictable way', and that, 'There *are* sex differences that create differences in the brain, [but] sex isn't the determining factor in brain development that it is for the reproductive system'. For which we can all be very grateful. Cordelia, too, is an interactionist.

It's no wonder that this middle ground has been hard to establish, or has become the stuff of culture wars. The wish to not acknowledge any biological brain differences at all is absolutely understandable. Within living memory, women were denied the vote, the right to own property, and to refuse sex from their husbands, and kept from positions of power or participation in many professions, sports, or economic activities. This outrageous gender apartheid persisted for thousands of years and blighted millions of lives. No wonder there is resistance to any idea that we might be different beings, most of us, along gender lines. Fear of turning back the clock is valid and natural. Yet progress depends on facing facts. It must be possible to have equality without insisting on sameness.

The evidence for gender differences grows each year. In 2017, the *Journal of Neuroscience Research* dedicated a whole edition to reporting on the hundreds of studies and examples that were emerging. Alan Schore's sweeping 2015 review, cited previously, focused on the unique vulnerability of the male brain *in utero* and in the first twelve months of life, and pretty much explained all the observable facts – the incarceration rates, suicidal tendencies, drug addiction, disposition to violence, school difficulties and behaviour disorders in which boys and men so predominate. Like climate change denial, gender denial simply cannot stand against the tide of evidence.

What has changed in our thinking is that the categories are not hard and fast. Once you abandon binary thinking and see gender as a continuum, then you don't talk about a male brain or a female brain, but you can allow degrees of masculinisation or feminisation. We all live on that line.

It's shocking how much this can matter. Take one example – the sleeping drug zolpidem, marketed as Ambien, has been used by millions around the world. During early testing, it was found that women metabolised the drug at half the speed of men. Their brains were still slowed down far into the next day, whereas men woke mostly free of its effects. But this was not made public for twenty years. Researchers believe that this may have led to as many as half a million premature deaths from vehicle accidents, falls in the elderly, and higher cancer rates.[9] That's a terrible price to pay for denying the existence of brain or body differences between women and men.

Finally, and on a much happier note, there is one other fact helping us understand gender's complex dance between biology and culture. The existence of people who are LGBTQI clearly shows that conditioning does not solely or finally determine us. The central understanding of alternate sexual identities is that people are 'born this way' and it's an essential part of who they are. If gender were not real, then transgender would not be real either, along with all the other variations that exist despite society's continual and oppressive pressure on us all to be the same. Gender is one of the delightful diversities of human beings, and if we can learn to manage it better from babyhood onwards, our boys and girls might live in a far happier world. To do that, we have to know the material we are working with, the unique biology of every single child, and then we can do our jobs as parents and teachers and human beings.

Warmly,
Steve Biddulph

Notes

1. Loveless, T., *Girls, Boys and Reading, The Brown Centre Report on American Education*, March 2015. You can read this online at https://www.brookings.edu/research/girls-boys-and-reading/. 'The origins of the gender gap are hotly debated. The universality of the gap certainly supports the argument that it originates in biological or developmental differences between the two sexes. It is evident among students of different ages in data collected at different points in time. It exists across the globe, in countries with different educational systems, different popular cultures, different child rearing practices, and different conceptions of gender roles. Moreover, the greater prevalence of reading impairment among young boys – a ratio of two or three to one – suggests an endemic difficulty that exists before the influence of schools or culture can take hold' [xiii].
2. Schore, A. N. (2017), 'All our sons: The developmental neurobiology and neuroendocrinology of boys at risk', *Infant Ment Health J*, Jan, 38, 1, 15–52. You can read this online at http://onlinelibrary.wiley.com/doi/10.1002/imhj.21616/full.
3. Deak, JoAnn, *How Girls Thrive*, Green Blanket Press, Columbus, Ohio, 2010.
4. Wilkinson, R. and Pickett, K., *The Spirit Level: Why Greater Equality Makes Societies Stronger*, Allen Lane, London, 2009.
5. Fine, Cordelia, *Testosterone Rex: Unmaking the Myths of Our Gendered Minds*, Norton, New York, 2017.
6. Fine, Cordelia, *Delusions of Gender: How Our Minds, Society and Neurosexism Create Differences*, Norton, New York, 2010.
7. McCarthy, Margaret M., Ball, Gregory F. (2011), 'Tempests and tales: challenges to the study of sex differences in the brain', *Biology of Sex Differences*, 2, 1, 4 ISSN 2042-6410. DOI:10.1186/2042-6410-2-4.

8. 'An Issue Whose Time Has Come: Sex/Gender Influences on Nervous System Function' (2017) *Journal of Neuroscience Research* 95, 1–2.

9. Lehmann, Claire, 'The XX factor: When gender differences are ignored in health studies, it's women who pay the price', *Commentary Magazine*, 15 March 2017.